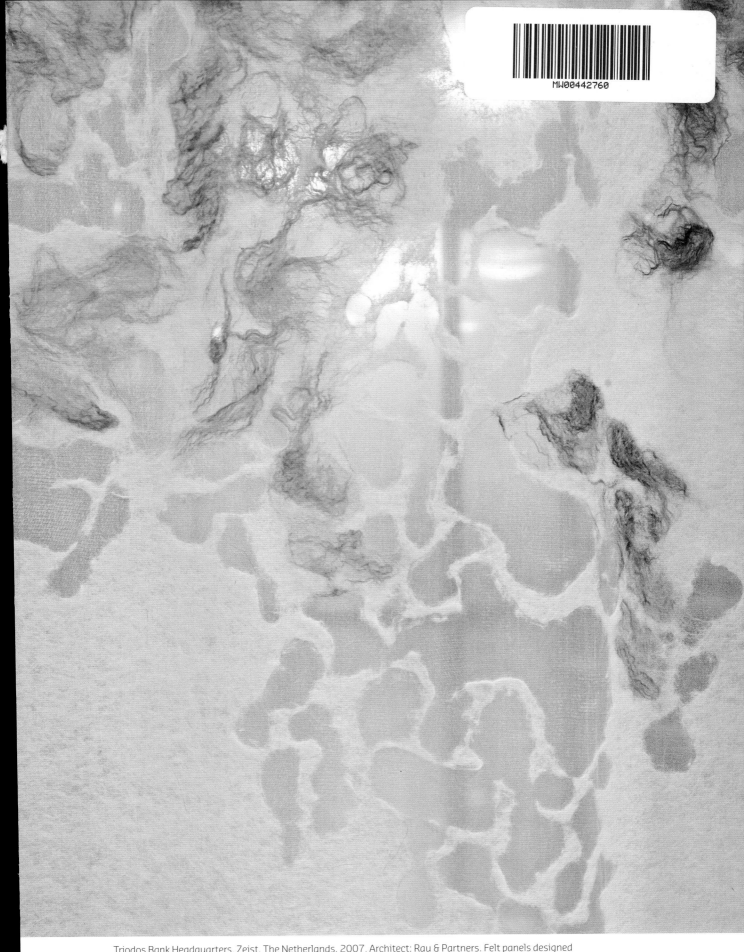

Triodos Bank Headquarters, Zeist, The Netherlands, 2007. Architect: Rau & Partners. Felt panels designed by Claudy Jongstra. Made by Studio Claudy Jongstra. Drenthe Heath, Wensleydale, and Merino wools, silk organza, raw silk. Photo: Peter Cuypers

Cover: Central Public Library, Amsterdam, the Netherlands, 2007. Architect: Jo Coenen & Co. Architekten. Felt walls designed by Claudy Jongstra. Made by Studio Claudy Jongstra. Drenthe Heath, Wensleydale, and Merino wools; raw silk. Photo: Peter Cuypers

Susan Brown
Andrew Dent
Christine Martens
Matilda McQuaid

FASHIONING FELT

Cell carpet strings. Designed by Yvonne Laurysen and Erik Mantel. Manufactured by LAMA Concept.
The Netherlands, 2004. Wool felt. Photo: LAMA Concept

Felt-making process, Hut Up, Berlin, Germany, 2008. Photo: Christine Birkle

Table of Contents

1. Fluid Green. Designed and made by Inge Lindqvist. Copenhagen, Denmark, 1998. Industrial wool felt, dyed by stitch-resist.
Cooper-Hewitt, National Design Museum, Smithsonian Institution, Museum purchase through gift of John Pierpont Morgan and Mrs. Hamilton Fish Webster
and from General Acquisitions Endowment Fund, 2008-17-1. Photo: Inge Lindqvist

Foreword

Cooper-Hewitt, National Design Museum's world-renowned Textiles department houses woven artifacts from Han dynasty China and ancient Egypt as well as high-tech metallic tulle used as radar decoys among its 30,000 objects. But amid such rare and sophisticated textiles lies an altogether more humble fabric: felt.

The *Fashioning Felt* exhibition is curated by Susan Brown, Assistant Curator in the Textiles department, with Matilda McQuaid, Deputy Curatorial Director and Head of Textiles. In their hands, *Fashioning Felt* uncovers felt's ancient, vernacular roots in Central Asia and studies the material's current applications in avant-garde fashion and design. From Mongolian nomadic dwellings to the concourses of international airports, and in our wonderfully rich exhibition and publication, felt displays its intrinsic tactile appeal and versatility. Susan, Christine Martens, and Material Connexion's Andrew Dent have contributed essays which combine to give a thorough examination not only of where felt has been, but also where it is poised to go in the future.

I extend my sincere gratitude to Maharam, whose generous support has made this exhibition possible. Additional funding has been provided by The Coby Foundation, Ltd., and the Mondriaan Foundation. The Claudy Jongstra installation was made possible thanks to support from Elise Jaffe and Jeffrey Brown. Additional support is provided by The Netherland-America Foundation and The Consulate General of Switzerland in New York. And as always, this publication is made possible in part by the Andrew W. Mellon Foundation.

At Cooper-Hewitt, thanks are due to Cara McCarty, Curatorial Director; Jocelyn Groom, Head of Exhibitions; and Chul R. Kim, Director of Publications. And finally, congratulations to exhibition designer Toshiko Mori Architect, exhibition graphics designer Tsang Seymour Design, and catalogue designer Pure+Applied, who have delivered a marvelously tactile and visually appealing installation and book.

Paul Warwick Thompson
Director

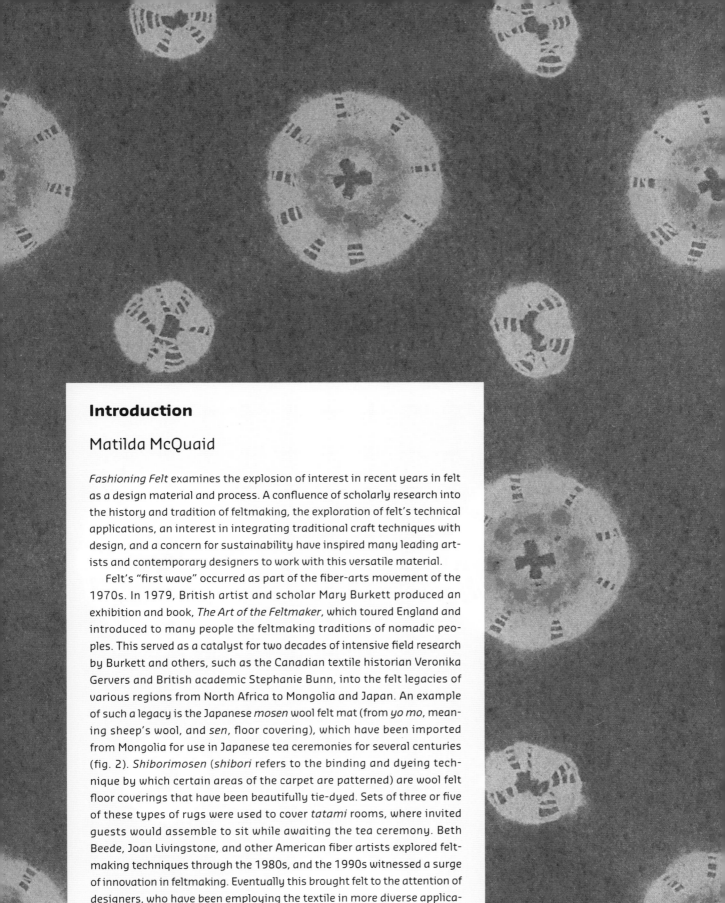

Introduction

Matilda McQuaid

Fashioning Felt examines the explosion of interest in recent years in felt as a design material and process. A confluence of scholarly research into the history and tradition of feltmaking, the exploration of felt's technical applications, an interest in integrating traditional craft techniques with design, and a concern for sustainability have inspired many leading artists and contemporary designers to work with this versatile material.

Felt's "first wave" occurred as part of the fiber-arts movement of the 1970s. In 1979, British artist and scholar Mary Burkett produced an exhibition and book, *The Art of the Feltmaker*, which toured England and introduced to many people the feltmaking traditions of nomadic peoples. This served as a catalyst for two decades of intensive field research by Burkett and others, such as the Canadian textile historian Veronika Gervers and British academic Stephanie Bunn, into the felt legacies of various regions from North Africa to Mongolia and Japan. An example of such a legacy is the Japanese *mosen* wool felt mat (from *yo mo*, meaning sheep's wool, and *sen*, floor covering), which have been imported from Mongolia for use in Japanese tea ceremonies for several centuries (fig. 2). *Shiborimosen* (*shibori* refers to the binding and dyeing technique by which certain areas of the carpet are patterned) are wool felt floor coverings that have been beautifully tie-dyed. Sets of three or five of these types of rugs were used to cover *tatami* rooms, where invited guests would assemble to sit while awaiting the tea ceremony. Beth Beede, Joan Livingstone, and other American fiber artists explored felt-making techniques through the 1980s, and the 1990s witnessed a surge of innovation in feltmaking. Eventually this brought felt to the attention of designers, who have been employing the textile in more diverse applications in interior design and fashion.

2. *Mosen*. Mongolia (for the Japanese market), late 19th century. Wool, felted and *shibori*-dyed. Cooper-Hewitt, National Design Museum, Smithsonian Institution, Museum purchase from General Acquisitions Endowment Fund, 2005-2-1. Photo: Matt Flynn

Due to its unique properties—it is fire-retardant and self-extinguishing; it dampens vibration and absorbs sound; and it can hold large amounts of fluid without feeling wet—felt has long been an important material for industrial and technical uses, including padding, insulation, and fluid transfer/management. Industrial felt is typically made from low-grade and recycled wool. Since its use by the German artist Joseph Beuys in the 1960s, it has occasionally been co-opted by designers for its soft yet unmistakably industrial quality. Danish textile designer Inge Lindqvist interprets industrial felt through the traditional stitch resist dyeing technique, which consists of stitching areas before immersion dyeing so as to retain the color of the base cloth (fig. 1). Lindqvist uses highly absorbent industrial felt that is folded, pleated, and stitched vertically, and then immerses each half of the felt separately into the dye. The "waterline" is depicted by the whiter areas on the felt.

In recent years, designers have experimented with high-quality industrial and handmade felt in more three-dimensional ways. It can be made thin and flexible or very dense and hard, and can be easily molded. Dutch jewelry designer Brigit Daamen felts fond mementos and cheap plastic costume jewelry with merino wool to reincarnate them into precious

3a. Windmills. Designed and made by Brigit Daamen. Haarlem, the Netherlands, 2003. Merino wool, Delft porcelain.
Photo: Brigit Daamen

3b. Necklace. Designed and made by Brigit Daamen. Haarlem, the Netherlands, 2003. Merino wool, coral. Photo: Brigit Daamen

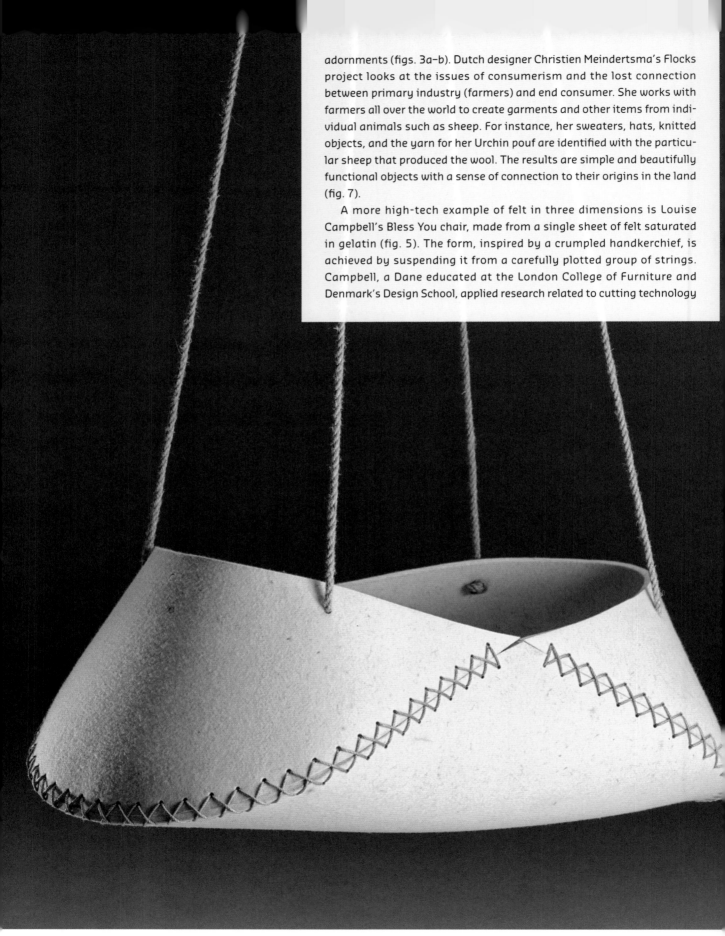

adornments (figs. 3a–b). Dutch designer Christien Meindertsma's Flocks project looks at the issues of consumerism and the lost connection between primary industry (farmers) and end consumer. She works with farmers all over the world to create garments and other items from individual animals such as sheep. For instance, her sweaters, hats, knitted objects, and the yarn for her Urchin pouf are identified with the particular sheep that produced the wool. The results are simple and beautifully functional objects with a sense of connection to their origins in the land (fig. 7).

A more high-tech example of felt in three dimensions is Louise Campbell's Bless You chair, made from a single sheet of felt saturated in gelatin (fig. 5). The form, inspired by a crumpled handkerchief, is achieved by suspending it from a carefully plotted group of strings. Campbell, a Dane educated at the London College of Furniture and Denmark's Design School, applied research related to cutting technology

4. Swing Low cradle. Designed by Søren Ulrick Petersen. Produced by SUP Design. Denmark, 1997. Wool felt, hemp rope. Photo: Erik Brahl

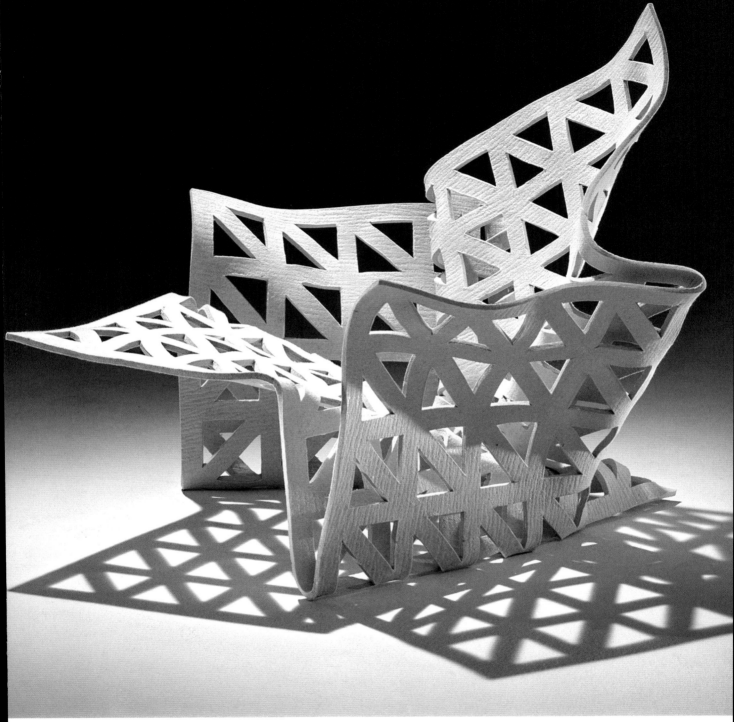

5. Bless You chair. Designed and made by Louise Campbell. Denmark, 1999. 10mm technical felt, 750 sheets of gelatin. Photo: Erik Brahl

from this prototype to later work, such as the Prince chair, which combines very personal expression with extreme engineering.

Another designer from Denmark's Design School who has taken advantage of felt's malleability is Søren Ulrik Petersen, who trained as a cabinetmaker. His Swing Low cradle, made for babies under two months, hangs from the ceiling or another stable structure (fig. 4). Rocking in a suspended cradle helps develop infants' motor skills and protects them from dirt, drafts, and pets. The dense wool felt shields the baby from ambient noise while creating a womb-like environment.

Felt also has a number of material and aesthetic characteristics that appeal to a broad range of designers, even those who do not normally work with textiles. Felt can be cleanly cut without fraying, and requires no finishing. It can be made from partially or fully recycled materials. Offcuts or by-products of some feltmaking processes can be reused or reinterpreted in other objects. Stephanie Odegard is the founder of Odegard, Inc., which specializes in hand-crafted rugs from Nepal, makes the embroidered Striped Felt runner (fig. 8). Remnants of cut edges from solid-color felt rugs are recovered, and the strips are hand-embroidered together to create a new carpet. Odegard employs artisans in developing countries such as India, allowing them to improve their quality of life and preserve their craft traditions. The Saba felt carpet (fig. 6), which uses a traditional technique called *ala kiiz*—in which a pattern is laid in the fiber state, typically resulting in blurred lines—is remarkable for the crispness of its lines and geometric design.

6. *Saba felt carpet. Designed by Stephanie Odegard. Manufactured by Rasheed for ODEGARD. India, 2007. Wool felt.* Photo: Odegard

7. Urchin poufs. Designed by Christien Meindertsma. Manufactured by Flocks. The Netherlands, 2007. Wool felt. Photo: Joost van Brug

Fashioning Felt presents an extraordinary range of felt. From two-dimensional carpets to three-dimensional environments, each work reveals the virtuosity of both the material and the designers. The exhibition and book focus on felt that has been produced by traditional hand- or machine-felting processes; they exclude other non-woven techniques, in order to underscore the essential elements of feltmaking—wool fiber, agitation, moisture, and pressure. The informative essays that follow discuss the seemingly limitless possibilities of felt as a medium in design, specifically in the contexts of tradition, craft, and technology. Christine Martens explains historic and current feltmaking traditions in Central Asia, recounting its communal and spiritual significance. Susan Brown discusses its applications in contemporary design while focusing on hand felters who maintain and reinterpret centuries-old feltmaking techniques. Andrew Dent writes about the technical properties of felt and of the industrial manufacturing processes that have led to innovative and iconic examples in contemporary design. The remarkable works featured in *Fashioning Felt* are true testaments to felt's longevity, and they are sure to inspire future generations of artists and designers.

8. Striped Felt carpet. Designed and manufactured by Rasheed for ODEGARD. India, 2007. Wool felt, cotton embroidery.
Photo: Odegard

1. Yurt with blue sink, Naryn, Kyrgyzstan, 2001. Photo: Janice Arnold

FELT
TRADITION

Christine Martens

2. Yurt interior, Kyrgyzstan, 2005. Photo: Saigan Ailchiev

Portable palaces and shepherd's cloaks, brilliant carpets and amulets, military helmets and quilted shields all have been fashioned of felt, the most humble of fabrics. Felt has been extolled in poems, proverbs, riddles, and blessings across a vast swath of Asia, symbolizing the sacred values of purity and strength for noblemen and nomads alike. Tangled masses of wool fibers, combined with only hot water and pressure—feltmaking is an art form which has persisted unchanged for millennia.

The history of feltmaking dates back the first century AD, in Northern Mongolia (*Noin Ula*), and still earlier to the frozen tundra of the Altai mountains of Siberia, where the contents of Pazyryk *kurgans*—stone burial vaults—from between the seventh and second centuries BC revealed extraordinary examples of felt along with clothing, jewelry, gold, silver, and ceramics. Elaborate ceremonial objects, such as a large scale hanging of a horse and rider approaching a seated deity, saddle pads embellished with gold, and sculptural swans are evidence of a well-developed felt tradition[1] and suggest felt's spiritual significance in these early nomadic communities, most likely the originators of the first felting processes.

From these early beginnings, feltmaking spread throughout the vast territory occupied by the Turkic-Mongolian tribes, extending from Anatolia in the west to the Gobi desert in the east and from the steppes of southern Russia to Central Asia in the south. These tribes lived on the wealth of their herds, mostly sheep and camels able to withstand harsh conditions and lengthy migrations from summer to winter pastures.[2] The distances they traveled varied, as did the terrain they traversed—from grassy steppe to wind-blown desert and perilous mountain ranges. Large herds were needed to produce the quantities of felt and skins needed for garments and shelters. The nomads lived in yurts, portable trellis-frame tents that were easily erected and dismantled (fig. 1). Their thick felt coverings, impervious to rain, snow, and wind, were quickly produced. "Tent furniture," often richly embellished with embroidery and appliqué in strong, vivid colors (fig. 2), typically included felt wall and floor coverings, bedding, hanging shelves, and bags for transport and storage. Ensuring that the yurts could withstand the rigors of nomadic life was often the responsibility of entire families. For the Turkic-Mongolian nomads, feltmaking was critical both to their culture and their survival. As historian B. Laufer noted, the material was "part and parcel of their lives and inseparable from their inward thoughts."[3]

Felt also possessed mystical and metaphorical qualities. At the installation as Chinggis Khan as ruler of all Turkic-Mongolian tribes in 1206, Sübe'etei Ba'adur, a trusted general in his army, made the following vow:

> Becoming like a covering felt
> I will try to give shelter
> Becoming like a wind-breaking felt
> I will try to protect the tent from the wind.[4]

3. *Three Dervishes*, V. V. Vereshagin, 1874. Painting's whereabouts unknown." Photo: Collection of the Peter the Great Museum of Anthropology and Ethnography (Kunstkamera), Russian Academy of Sciences, No. I-674-196

4. Khaksari dervish hat. Iran, first half 20th century. Wool felt, cotton embroidery. The Textile Museum, Ruth Lincoln Fisher Memorial Fund, 1985.16.1

5a. Jangyl Alibekova fluffing fleece with a willow branch, At-bashy, Kyrgyzstan, 2001. Photo: Christine Martens

Giovanni de Plano Carpini, a Franciscan friar sent by Pope Innocent IV as ambassador to the Mongols in the thirteenth century, encountered felt idols which flanked the entries of nomadic dwellings. The nomads looked upon them as amulets or guardians of the yurt's inhabitants and their herds—the essential source of their wealth[5]—and offered these figures a portion of their food and drink to ensure prosperity.[6] One custom was to hang a felt sky totem of a horse from a rope above the hearth in the yurt; and in remote areas of Mongolia today, families still practice the ancient ritual of hanging totems of humans riding foxes above the cradle of newborns in order to bring sweet dreams.[7]

The belief system of the early Turkic-Mongolian pastoralists encompassed both animism and shamanism and included the worship of Tengri, the great god of the sky, and Umai, a sacred female figure linked to the cult of fertility.[8] They and a multitude of other divinities and spirits are still embraced by Kyrgyz, Kazakhs, Turkmens, and Uzbeks. Islam was introduced in the eighth to tenth centuries, but it was the wandering Sufi dervishes (fig. 3), with their mystical practices and knowledge of pre-Islamic beliefs, who were able to convey the power and meaning of Islam

5b. Fluffing fleece on box spring, Naryn, Kyrgyzstan, 2001. Photo: Janice Arnold

6. Jangyl Alibekova dyeing wool, At-bashy, Kyrgyzstan, 2001. Photo: Christine Martens

in ways meaningful to the local populations.[9] Hats worn by dervishes required exacting construction and held symbolic significance. The *sikke*, a conical, honey-colored felt hat, is still worn by dervishes today as part of the costume worn when performing the *sema*, the ritual whirling dance. Made from the fleece of a young camel, it symbolizes the tombstone of man (fig. 4).[10]

In adjoining sedentary regions, female mullahs, viewed as healers, conducted ceremonies accompanying life-cycle traditions and were thought to have the power to solve problems such as infertility, illness, and poverty.[11] The nomadic communities, however, addressed these difficulties by venerating the graves of holy ancestors, Muslim saints, and legendary heroes through an active, local pilgrimage tradition (*ziyarat*), a critical element of Central Asian Islam today.[12]

Nomadic tribes were also fearless warriors, hunters, and traders. As they traveled along the legendary trade routes between China and Europe, cross-pollination with sedentary traders took place, and they transmitted feltmaking to the settled Uzbek population; the Lakai, of southern Uzbekistan, produced pieced felts similar to those of the Kyrgyz and Kazakhs.[13] This interaction impacted local customs as well as material culture, and influenced figurative representations in pattern, which were most often highly abstracted zoomorphic, botanical, and cosmological images.

The Kyrgyz, Kazakhs, Turkmen, and Lakai were among the peoples annexed by Russia in the nineteenth century and brutally collectivized by Stalin in the 1930s. The Soviets suppressed all forms of religious and mystical belief, viewing it as an impediment to modernization. The practice of many crafts was also banned, but continued clandestinely. Although migration ceased for the most part in the early twentieth century, the peoples of Central Asia have fiercely maintained their ancient nomadic customs. Felts encountered today in the region's homes and markets, mostly carpets and pillows, retain characteristics of the original tradition: highly abstract compositions, powerful rhythmic lines, and accentuated positive and negative space (fig. 16). Many permanent dwellings of the Kyrgyz and Kazakhs have one room brilliantly arrayed with *shyrdaks* and *ala kiiz*, the two basic types of felt carpet.

Making Felt

The traditional feltmaking process in this region begins with the fall sheep shearing. The fleece is washed and dried, the fibers are separated by being beaten and turned on two long, flexible wood (often tamarisk) or metal rods, on the dried skin of a foal, or on an old Russian bedspring, through which the dirt and plant debris fall (figs. 5a–b).[14] Dyeing was originally carried out with natural dyestuffs (fig. 6); but synthetic dyes became more prevalent after their introduction at the beginning of the twentieth century (fig. 7).

Large mats made of locally gathered reeds are constructed with a twining technique similar to basketry. The twining cords are weighted with chunks of wood or stone and tossed back and forth as each new piece of reed is added (figs. 8a–b). Fluffed and separated fleece is laid out in layers on the mat until the desired thickness is attained. Hot water is

7. Chemical dyes in the bazaar, Mary, Turkmenistan, 2008. Photo: Christine Martens

carefully poured on the fleece, which is then rolled up tightly in the reed mat, tied securely, and wrapped in heavy plastic. A long rope is looped around the roll. As one person holds the two ends of the rope and, walking backward, guides its movement, neighbors, including men and children, kick the roll forward along the ground (fig. 9). Alternately, the roll can be pulled by a donkey, horse, or camel. Rolling provides the agitation needed to compact and shrink the fleece. After several hours, it is unrolled, re-rolled from the opposite end, and wetted again.

The final stage, known as fulling, is accomplished by a group of women on their knees, with the newly felted piece rolled tightly in front of them (fig. 10). Working in rhythm and bearing down with their arms, they roll the felt back and forth on itself, causing it to harden and shrink further. The women re-roll the felt from the opposite end and repeat the process, as the shrinkage occurs in the direction of the rolling. Toward the end, one woman stands in the center of the rolled felt, while her companions on either side slam the felt against the ground, providing additional friction and pressure. The fulling continues until the desired shape, hardness, and size are achieved.

8a. Reeds for making reed mats, Mary, Turkmenistan, 2008. Photo: Christine Martens

8b. Constructing a reed mat, Mary, Turkmenistan, 2008. Photo: Christine Martens

9. Jangyl Alibekova and neighbors "kicking" the felt, At-bashy, Kyrgyzstan, 2001. Photo: Christine Martens

The construction of the shyrdak, a richly ornamented mosaic carpet, begins with solid-colored sheets of felt. Two pieces in contrasting colors are simultaneously cut with a knife or scissors into a traditional pattern, then reassembled with the positive of the first color set into the negative of the alternate color (figs. 11a–c). They are sewn together, with hand-spun cords covering the seams. The entire piece is backed with one large piece of felt and quilted together, with a woolen thread in rows of running stitches that echo the lines of the design (fig. 12). Traditionally made as part of a girl's trousseau and passed down from mother to daughter, shyrdaks are now made for sale and have become popular at regional craft fairs (fig. 13).[15] Ala kiiz, translated as "bright felt," is another method of patterning felt. Fleece that has already been dyed a variety of colors is laid out in a pattern on a reed screen and felted as outlined above.

In Turkmenistan, the intricate pattern is laid out on the screen with lengths of fleece that have been lightly spun and subsequently filled in with a variety of colored fibers. A wider border of natural black fleece is often added to the design with a backing of gray or white wool of lesser quality. After the pattern construction is completed, the fleece is rolled in the reed screen, securely tied, set on end; hot water is poured onto the top of the roll in order to saturate the fibers. Two ropes are passed around the enclosed fleece and reed screen, and two people standing on either side pull the roll back and forth. In the final step, kneeling women bear down with their arms and slam the felt against the ground until the fulling process is complete (figs. 14a–d). Turkmen felts appear to have a gentle haze that somewhat blurs the pattern, a result of the white or light gray fleece of the back side migrating through to the front pattern during the felting process. Feltmakers from the Mary region do not feel that a carpet is complete until they have re-felted it one year after the initial construction.[16] Patterns, which in the past indicated tribal affiliation and region, contain many references to the sun, plants, and animals. Ram's horns, frequently found hanging over a dwelling entrance or sculpted in relief on outdoor clay ovens as an ancient symbol of strength and protection, are represented in numerous configurations. In Turkmen folklore, snakes are respected for their connection to water sources, and, despite the negative connotations of snakes in Islam and Zoroastrianism, they are portrayed in the prayer rugs of mountainous Garrygala, in western Turkmenistan.[17] The Yomut of the Balkan region decorate the backside of the felt as well. They are known for very large felts called *ojak bashi*,[18] which are made specifically for yurts. A rectangular section indicated by the pattern is cut out and flipped back, making room for the hearth in the center of the yurt.

Before the Soviet period, felts were also used extensively for donkey, horse, and camel trappings (figs. 15a–b) as well as for hammock-like cradles suspended from the struts of the yurt. They are now used primarily as carpets and as padding for the large, raised outdoor wooden structures (*tapchan*) where meals and tea are consumed in the warmer months. Felt prayer rugs (*namazlyk*), made with white fleece of higher quality than

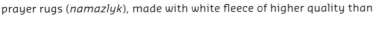

10. Jangyl Alibekova fulling the felt, At-bashy, Kyrgyzstan, 2005. Photo: Christine Martens

11a–c. Cutting patterns from two layers of felt for shyrdak, Kyrgyzstan, 2001. Photo: Janice Arnold

12. Hand-stitching the shyrdak, Kyrgyzstan, 2001. Photo: Janice Arnold

that of ordinary carpets, are in the shape of a *mihrab*, the curved niche in every mosque indicating the direction of Mecca. Namazlyk often feature a colored pattern of a tree of life (*daragt*) or ram's horns. A small area made of camel wool indicates the place where the head touches the carpet during prayer. Camels are held in high regard in Turkmenistan, and their fleece is believed to generate a sacred power force.[19] Triangular amulets (*doga*), both worn and hung, are also made of felt and decorated with embroidery.

While typically a domestic or village activity, feltmaking was also undertaken on a larger scale. As today, the efficiency of tent dwelling was exploited by the military. In the twelfth and thirteenth centuries, craftsmen assembled from all parts of the vast Mongolian kingdom produced the large quantities of felt necessary for the Mongols' continuous military campaigns. The Ottoman army used yurts extensively, for shelter and ceremonial purposes. Felt boots and headgear, in particular those of the sultan's elite Janissary corps, were crucial components of the Ottoman military uniform, and the highly organized army included artisans to provide necessary repairs.[20]

Felt in Turkey

Felts have not been well preserved in Turkey as they were considered of little cultural significance. But the writings of the seventeenth-century Turkish travel writer Evliya Celebi record many practical uses for felt. In the palace at Bitlis, lemons and oranges were preserved in winter by wrapping them in felt[21]; and, in Amasya, near Tokat, felt was used as a strainer for mulberry, grape, and quince juices.[22] In Erzerum, where winters were long and houses built of stone, felt and canvas treated with beeswax served as insulation under the roof.[23] In Bursa, during the month of July, the snow sellers brought ice wrapped in felt to the cities on mules. They also transported ice in felt bags for the court kitchens, harem, and Grand Vizier in Istanbul.[24] Evliya also describes the clothing of the men making canons in the arsenal, who wore felt clothing to save their bodies from the "blazes of hell."[25]

Mystical craft guilds, known as *ahi*,[26] in Ottoman Turkey oversaw the production and quality of felt and the behavior of its makers. In Istanbul alone, the feltmakers' guild had 400 workshops and more than 1,000 members.[27] Of guild regulations, we know only that the apprentices (*cirak*) were not permitted to smoke or sit cross-legged in the presence of a master; masters were not permitted to steal apprentices from colleagues' workshops; and masters were to present garments to their journeymen during important religious feasts.[28] When an apprentice was ready to open his own shop, the masters were invited to a juried event, at which the apprentice demonstrated the making of a shepherd's coat, prepared a meal for the judges, and gave a bar of olive oil soap to all in attendance.[29] The *Surname* (*Book of Festivities*) of Murad III, a manuscript of text and miniature paintings, commemorates the circumcision of Crown Prince Mehmet in Istanbul in 1582. The imperial celebration lasted for fifty-two days and nights and included a procession of the Istanbul guilds. The manuscript states, "The feltmakers were dressed

13. Festival market with shyrdak carpets, Naryn, Kyrgyzstan, 2001. Photo: Christine Martens

14. Mary, Turkmenistan, 2008. Photos: Christine Martens
a) Feltmaker laying out pattern with roving and fleece; b) Filling in the border with black fleece;

c) Fulling the felted carpet with forearms; d) Hardening the felt

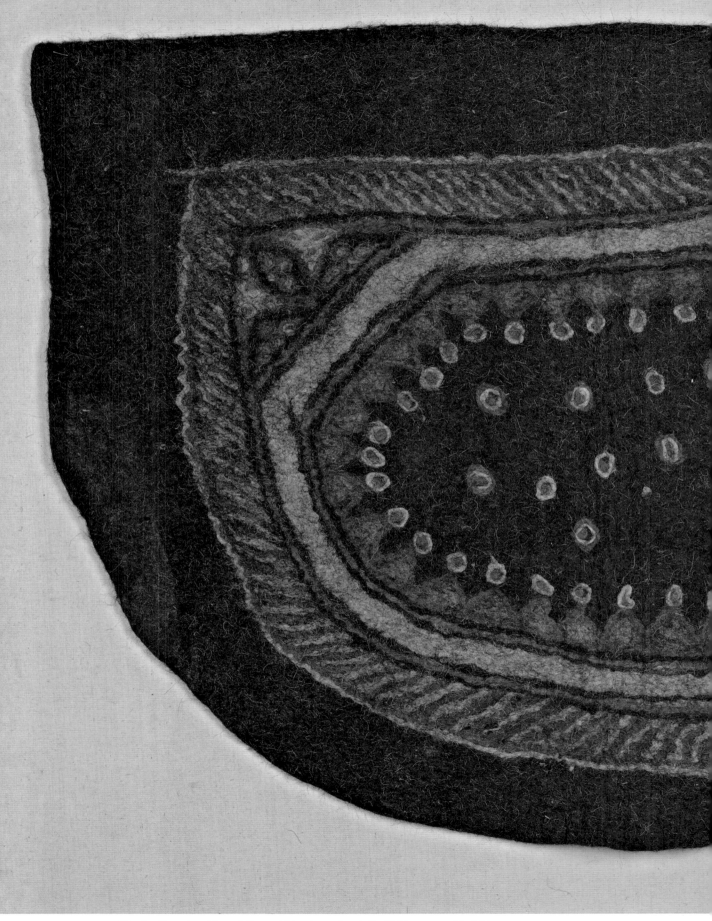

15a. Jat (Gypsy) saddle pad. Herat, Afghanistan, first half of 20th century. Wool felt.
American Museum of Natural History, 70.2/4666

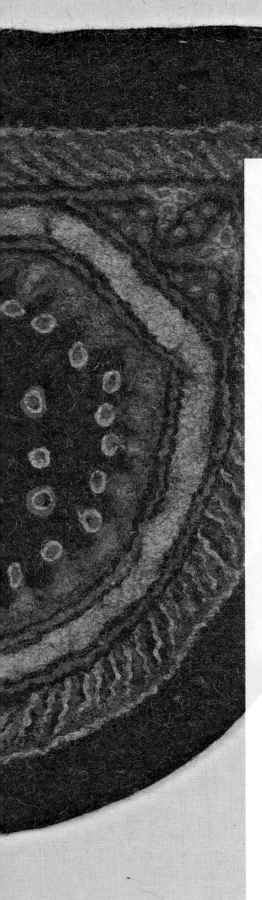

in bizarre and fearsome costumes with robes and turbans made (made both inside and out) of colored felt. They also pulled behind them a figure of a lion fashioned of felt."[30]

Many Turkish baths (*hamamlar*) had designated areas dedicated to felt production, as their extreme heat and moisture provided an ideal environment for feltmaking, especially during the winter months. The craftsman placed his felt on raised platforms and exerted pressure by pounding his chest on the fleece in order to achieve the necessary shrinkage. The last hamamlar that produced felt were in Konya and Urfa; by the last quarter of the twentieth century, many hand-felting processes were replaced by machines. Today, in the wool bazaar of Konya, fleece is washed in vast pools of water, aided by a mechanized, rake-like fork that agitates the fibers, before they are rinsed and hung to dry. Carding—the aligning and separating of fibers—was originally done by hand, but is now accomplished by a machine with large steel teeth, that combs the fibers as they are fed through.

In a hybrid of the two methods of patterning felt previously mentioned, Anatolian craftsmen use partially felted fabric of varying colors called "pre-felt" to cut the patterns that form the decorative elements of the carpet, resulting in a more clearly defined design than ala khiz (fig. 17). Once the pre-felt elements are laid in position on the reed mat, they are covered evenly with the background fleece using a forked tool of cherry wood called a *çubuk* (fig. 18). Additional layers of fleece follow, each sprinkled with water through a long-fibered straw brush before being rolled in the reed mat, wrapped in plastic, and sent to a mechanical "kicking" machine for hardening, the first stage of the shrinkage process. Here it is turned and pounded for three hours, or "kicked" by the

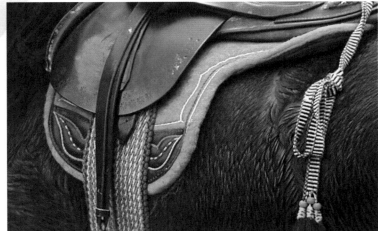

15b. Saddle pad, Tire, Turkey, 2003. Photo: Christine Martens

feltmakers, who rhythmically roll the felt forward with their right foot and backward with their left, hands on their knees for pressure. Upon completion, the pre-felt patterns are firmly felted to the fleece of the background.

Next, the rug is unrolled, the edges are trimmed, and the pattern is adjusted before it is placed in a steaming machine for the fulling. The rug is steamed, turned, and compressed, with olive oil soap used as a sizing agent. Every twenty minutes, the rug is removed and re-rolled both inside out and back to front to ensure even felting. This process continues for six hours, which causes shrinkage of forty percent and makes the felt impervious to moisture. While it is a dwindling tradition, feltmaking workshops in Konya, Afyon, Tire, Balikesir, Urfa, and Mardin still produce shepherd's cloaks and carpets (fig. 21).

In Mongolia, which borders Kazakhstan in the east and China in the west, approximately sixty percent of the population are herders and still live in yurts (*ger*). (figs. 19a–c) The ger is also the traditional environment for sacred rituals, attesting to the significance of this traditional architectural form in Mongol culture.[31] A chance encounter with sheep shearers necessitates the offering of a blessing:

> May your shorn wool
> Become like a mountain
> And your scissors blunt

To which is replied, "May your blessings come to pass."[32]

Unlike Central Asian felt carpets, Mongol felts are typically white, sometimes with a red border. In traditional oral poetry and lore, white is an auspicious color, denoting purity and strength.[33] Peter Andrews suggests that, although there is no particular rule regarding the usage of white felt for tents, legend states that the tomb of Chinggis Khan was associated with eight white trellis tents, and ancient travelers also noted that white was the color of choice.[34] Today, as in the past, the central field of most felt carpets is white, and embroidery, which continues to play an important role in the embellishment of the felt, is done with camel hair (figs. 20a–d). Simple geometric designs form the structure on which more complex patterns are constructed and derive from early patterns that represented animals or their body parts. Interlocking patterns and wavelike designs are but a few of the myriad forms that symbolize a wish for large families and herds as well as good health and happiness.[35]

Feltmaking in Mongolia can be divided into two categories: large-scale production by families working communally in the fall, and small-scale production in individual homes done year round. While the basic feltmaking technique is the same as elsewhere in Central Asia, there are many customs unique to Mongolia. The *khotlogch*, or director of the feltmaking ritual, oversees the entire process. When the fleece is laid out and the roll bound, a blessing is recited:

> Become hard
> Like the head of a bull
> Become stiff
> Like the neck of a camel.[36]

At this time, a woman sprinkles fermented mare's milk over the felt and milk over the head of the horse that will pull the felt, while dried juniper branches are burned to purify both felt and horse.[37] These and many

16. Carpet. Uzbek, Afghanistan, mid-20th century. Wool, felted, pieced, and hand-sewn. Textile Museum of Canada, Opekar/Webster Collection, T94.2204

other rituals are meant to bring good fortune to the makers and special qualities to the felt. Certain taboos also exist: All participants must display utter respect toward one another and avoid words of anger or conflict, lest harm come not only to the felt but also to the family. The saying "While among others, check your tongue; while alone, check your mind" demonstrates the Mongol desire for harmony in all actions.[38]

When the felt is completed, there is a large celebration (*esgiin khutaar*), at which food is served and words of wisdom offered by the elders. Along with singing and dancing, riddles are solved by opposing teams, and legends and epic poems are recited long into the night within the candlelit yurt.[39] At the end of the ritual, there are calls for rain; it is said that when poems, epics and songs are performed well, rain and snow will follow.[40]

During the Soviet period, small-scale felt production by Mongol herders was replaced by a factory-based system, and the ancient customs of feltmaking, embroidery, and quilting were abandoned. Since Mongolia's establishment as an independent sovereign republic in 1991, however, some herders have returned to traditional production. The collapse of the Soviet Union in 1991 unexpectedly thrust independence upon Central Asia, leaving the entire area to face harsh economic and political

17. "Pre-felt" cut into pattern shapes, Mehmet Gircic workshop, Konya, Turkey, 2001. Photo: Christine Martens

18. Mehmet Gircic laying the fleece over the pre-felt design, Mehmet Gircic workshop, Konya, Turkey, 2001. Photo: Christine Martens

19a–c. Herders making felt in Terelj, Mongolia, 2008. Photos: Christine Martens

20a–d. Traditional felt quilting at a women's cooperative in Altanbulag, Mongolia, 2008. Photos: Christine Martens

challenges and questions of national identity. Aid to Artisans (ATA), a nonprofit organization in Hartford, Connecticut, supported by the U.S. Agency for International Development (USAID), has embarked on a four-year program in Kazakhstan, Uzbekistan, Kyrgyzstan, Tajikistan, and Turkmenistan to keep alive regional artistic traditions, materials, and techniques. Through workshops and roundtable discussions, ATA helped artisans learn about making their wares available in international markets, giving craftsmen, especially women, resources and earning power.

The ongoing adaptability of nomadic peoples to their environment has contributed to the resilience of their feltmaking. Their intimate relationship with nature is evident in their designs portraying suns and moons, scorpions and ram's horns, flora and fauna. These patterns have undergone many transformations in form and meaning through the mingling and migrating of tribes and through political upheaval. But the nomadic philosophy of life, in which the artisan is a steward of the land and its creatures, provides us with an enduring, beautiful legacy in felt.

21. Kepeneks (shepherd's cloaks) being sold on the street with vegetables, Tire, Turkey, 2003.
Photo: Christine Martens

Drenthe Heath sheep. Photo: Jeroen Musch

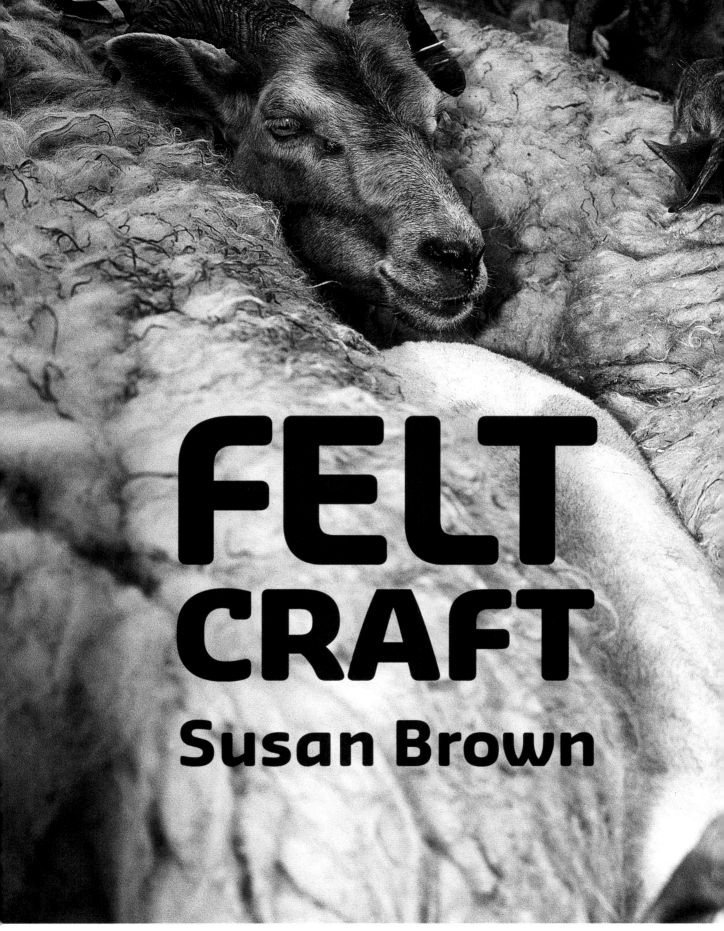

FELT
CRAFT
Susan Brown

1. A–Z Fiber Form: White Dress. Designed and made by Andrea Zittel. United States, 2002. Wool, felted, skirt pins. *Courtesy of the artist and Andrea Rosen Gallery, New York. Photo: Kentaro Takioka*

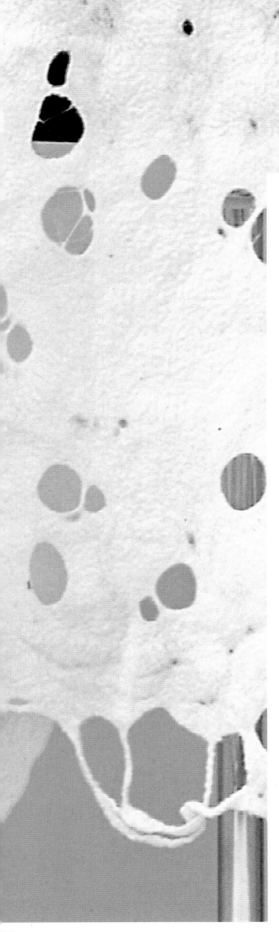

Felt feels like something that exists in nature. Although it is manufactured both by hand and by machine, felt has the gravitas of a raw material, such as wood or stone. Its dense, fibrous texture inspires an almost primal sense of comfort and protection. Felt is made from wool, a traditional textile fiber, but it is very different from other materials. Most textiles begin as string: fiber, whatever the source, is aligned and spun to form long, consistent strands. Woven fabrics, along with knitting, crochet, and lace, are the result of rules applied to string. Like music, these textiles have a mathematical beauty, an internal structure based on repetition and variation. Felt, on the other hand, is, according to Kenneth Hayes, "that singular fabric that capitulates to the natural tendency of fibers to entangle."[1] Rather than being built up stitch by stitch and row by row, the whole woolly mass is laid out at once, and then transformed into something different through the vigorous application of soap, water, and energy. Felt is disorderly, entropic, full of trapped energy. Perhaps that is why the experience of touching it is so affecting.

The immediacy of felt, its fundamental difference, was instinctively arrived at by Andrea Zittel through her *A–Z Personal Uniform Series*. Zittel, a California-based artist whose creations are typically experiments in living, explores means of self-determination in the face of socially constructed needs. In 1991, tired of the constant variety in apparel demanded by the social etiquette of the workplace, she conceived the *A–Z Six Month Uniform*. She designed one perfect black dress per season, had it made by a professional seamstress, and wore it every day until the next seasonal creation. After a few years, she shifted her focus to the planar nature of textiles, opting for garments made only from rectangles which she could sew herself (*A–Z Personal Panel Uniform*, 1995–98), and later only from rectangles literally torn from the bolt (*A–Z Raugh Uniform*, 1998). The concept naturally reverted to the threads from which those textiles were woven. She crocheted dresses from a single string (*Single Strand Uniforms*, 1998–2001) and, in a further refinement, learned to manipulate the strand using only her fingers, eliminating even the single rudimentary tool required for crochet.

For ten years, Zittel's uniform concept had been evolving toward purer ways of making. Then, in 2002, she discovered felting. "Now I am finally beginning to make the most direct form of clothing possible by hand-felting wool directly into the shape of a garment," states Zittel.[2] Her seamless dresses are formed directly from fiber in three dimensions, with all variation of color, shape, and ornament executed during the felt-making process (fig. 1). Fascinated by the flexibility of the technique, she quickly exceeded her strict seasonal requirements. Zittel includes these fiber uniforms in her *A–Z Advanced Technologies* projects, inviting the question of what sophistication truly means in the making of things.

Many have tried to describe a similar paradox in the work of Dutch designer Claudy Jongstra, whose felt textiles are prized precisely because they maintain so much of the character of the sheep: they seem to have been skinned rather than shorn, and the fleece laboriously worked into cloth. Through much of history, animals woven or embroidered onto textiles embodied wealth and power, but today, they have lost their symbolic status, and are largely limited to cartoon versions on children's textiles. Jongstra's felts, on the other hand, remain startlingly close to their animal source, and succeed in bringing the ancient apotropaic force—the ability to avert evil—of the animal to contemporary design.

2. Claudy Jongstra dyeing wool, Spannum, the Netherlands, 2008. Photo: Peter Cuypers

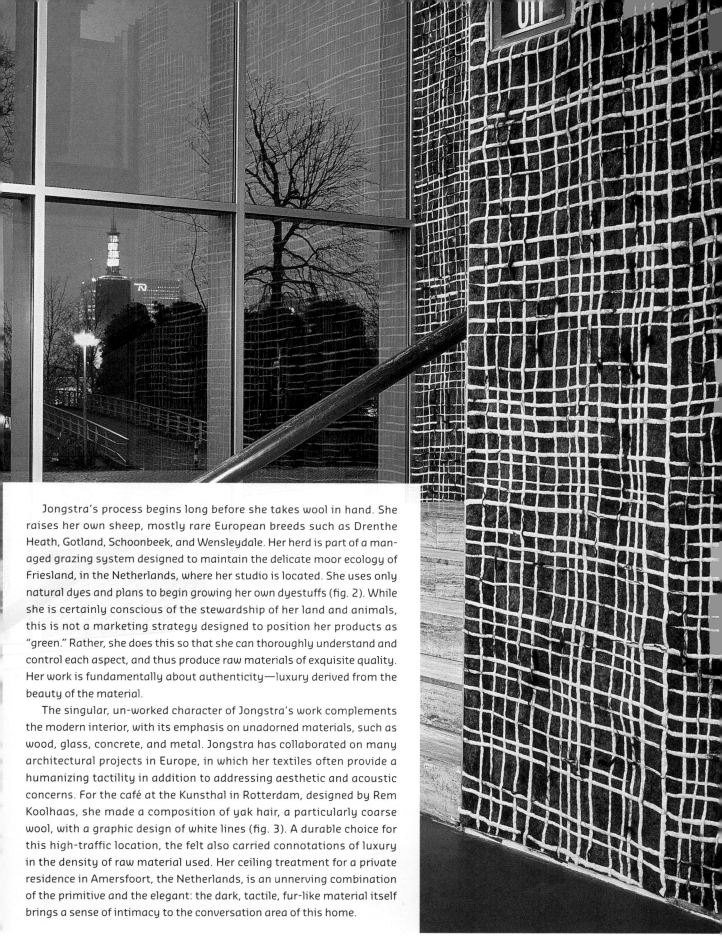

Jongstra's process begins long before she takes wool in hand. She raises her own sheep, mostly rare European breeds such as Drenthe Heath, Gotland, Schoonbeek, and Wensleydale. Her herd is part of a managed grazing system designed to maintain the delicate moor ecology of Friesland, in the Netherlands, where her studio is located. She uses only natural dyes and plans to begin growing her own dyestuffs (fig. 2). While she is certainly conscious of the stewardship of her land and animals, this is not a marketing strategy designed to position her products as "green." Rather, she does this so that she can thoroughly understand and control each aspect, and thus produce raw materials of exquisite quality. Her work is fundamentally about authenticity—luxury derived from the beauty of the material.

The singular, un-worked character of Jongstra's work complements the modern interior, with its emphasis on unadorned materials, such as wood, glass, concrete, and metal. Jongstra has collaborated on many architectural projects in Europe, in which her textiles often provide a humanizing tactility in addition to addressing aesthetic and acoustic concerns. For the café at the Kunsthal in Rotterdam, designed by Rem Koolhaas, she made a composition of yak hair, a particularly coarse wool, with a graphic design of white lines (fig. 3). A durable choice for this high-traffic location, the felt also carried connotations of luxury in the density of raw material used. Her ceiling treatment for a private residence in Amersfoort, the Netherlands, is an unnerving combination of the primitive and the elegant: the dark, tactile, fur-like material itself brings a sense of intimacy to the conversation area of this home.

3. Kunsthal, Rotterdam, the Netherlands, 2005. Architect: Rem Koolhaas. Felt wall designed by Claudy Jongstra. Made by Studio Claudy Jongstra. Yak hair, Drenthe Heath and Merino wools, cotton gauze. Photo: Jeroen Musch

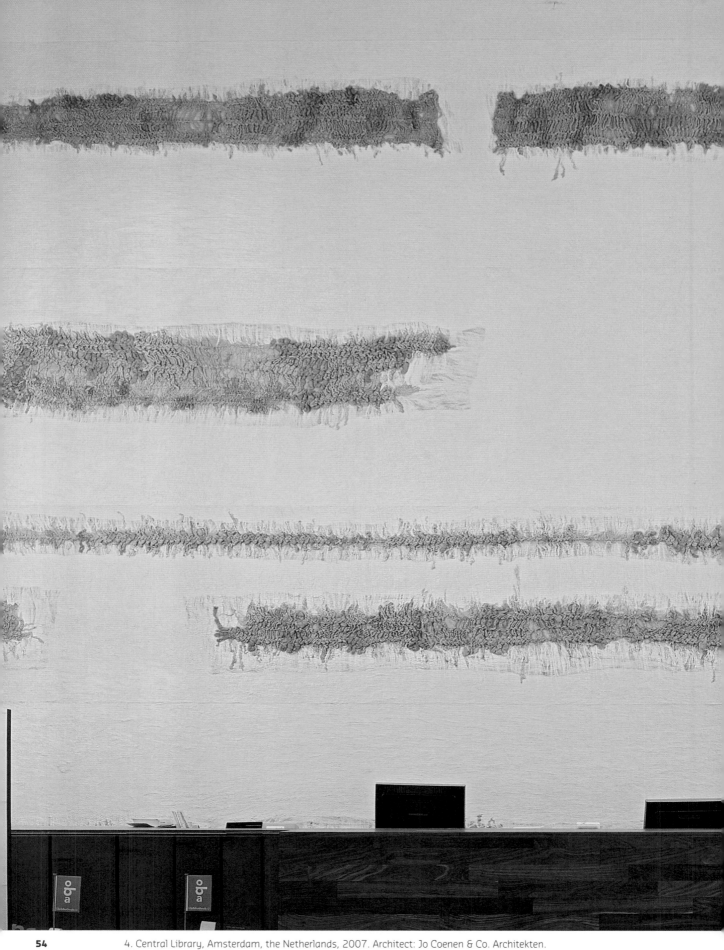

4. Central Library, Amsterdam, the Netherlands, 2007. Architect: Jo Coenen & Co. Architekten.
Felt walls designed by Claudy Jongstra. Made by Studio Claudy Jongstra. Drenthe Heath, Wensleydale,
and Merino wools; raw silk. Photo: Peter Cuypers

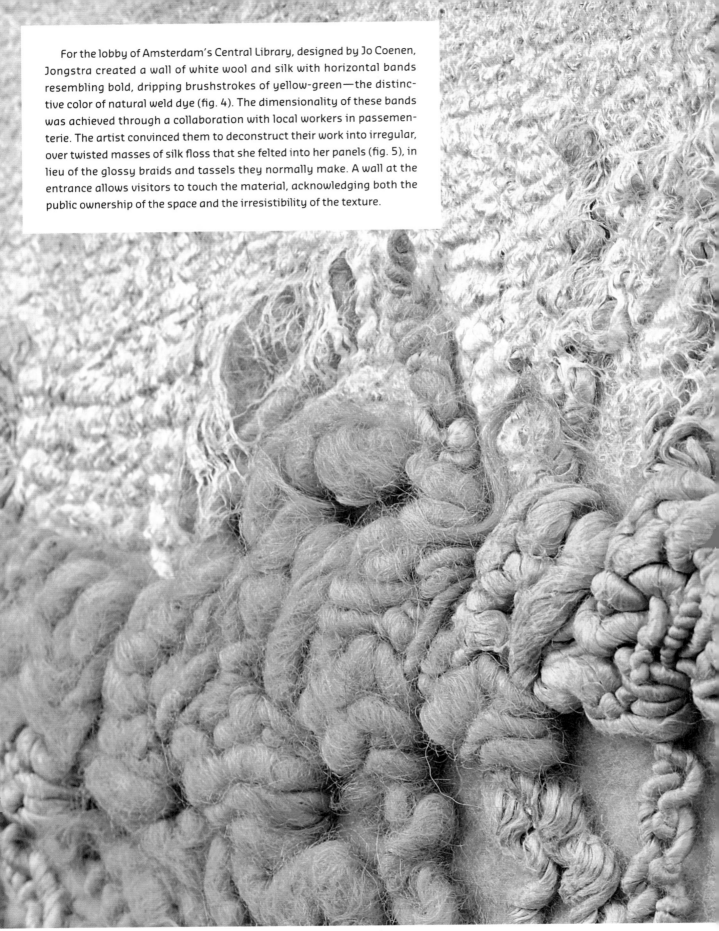

For the lobby of Amsterdam's Central Library, designed by Jo Coenen, Jongstra created a wall of white wool and silk with horizontal bands resembling bold, dripping brushstrokes of yellow-green—the distinctive color of natural weld dye (fig. 4). The dimensionality of these bands was achieved through a collaboration with local workers in passementerie. The artist convinced them to deconstruct their work into irregular, over twisted masses of silk floss that she felted into her panels (fig. 5), in lieu of the glossy braids and tassels they normally make. A wall at the entrance allows visitors to touch the material, acknowledging both the public ownership of the space and the irresistibility of the texture.

5. Central Library, Amsterdam, the Netherlands, 2007 (detail). Photo: Peter Cuypers

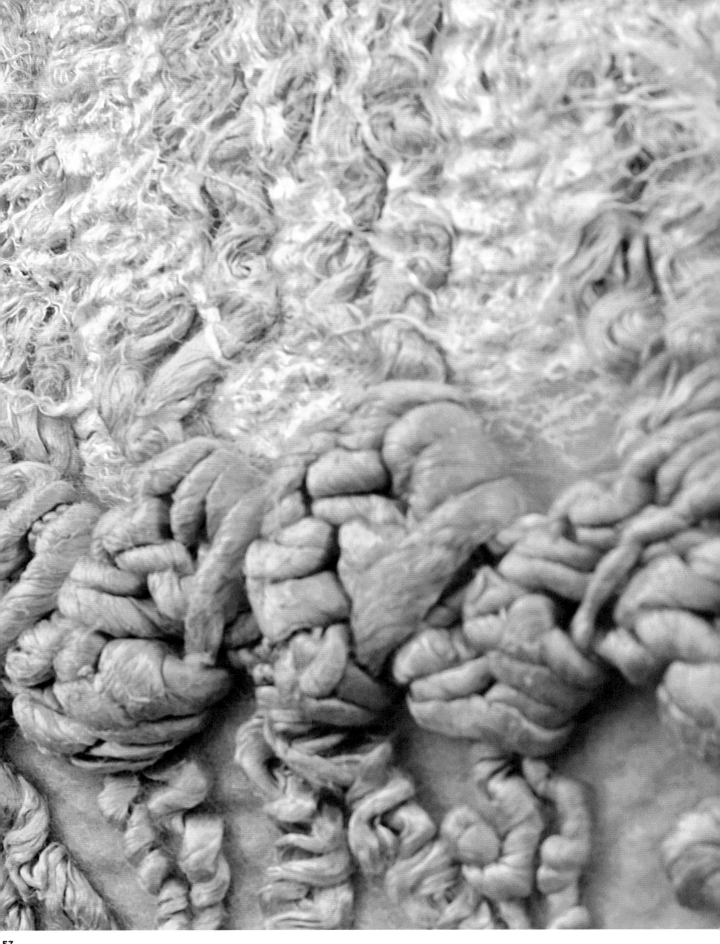

In other projects, most notably the council chamber at the House for Culture and Administration in Hellendoor, by Claus and Kaan Architects, Jongstra has focused on using textiles to define space. This room is entirely covered in unruly blue felt on the outside and pearly white wool and silk felts on the inside, and provides a private, quiet space for meeting or weddings in the middle of a busy indoor plaza. At the headquarters of Triodos Bank, designed by Rau and Partners, in Zeist, the Netherlands, Jongstra combined wool and silk felt with sheer silk cloth, enabling her to control the opacity (fig. 6). She applied the fibers selectively to provide customized privacy while maintaining the sense of openness and light originally planned for this glass interior (fig. 7). These installations feature textiles not as works of art commissioned to adorn public spaces, but as architectural materials which serve specific technical and aesthetic functions.

Felt has a unique history as a medium both for craft and for industry. It has incredible range—thin and translucent, very dense and thick, or even hard. It can be made in sheets or formed into three-dimensional shapes. The process of making felt and the tools and techniques used to manipulate it are different than for other textiles, and this invites designers to experiment with alternative approaches. Its plasticity is enabling a shift in the relationship of textiles to architecture and design.

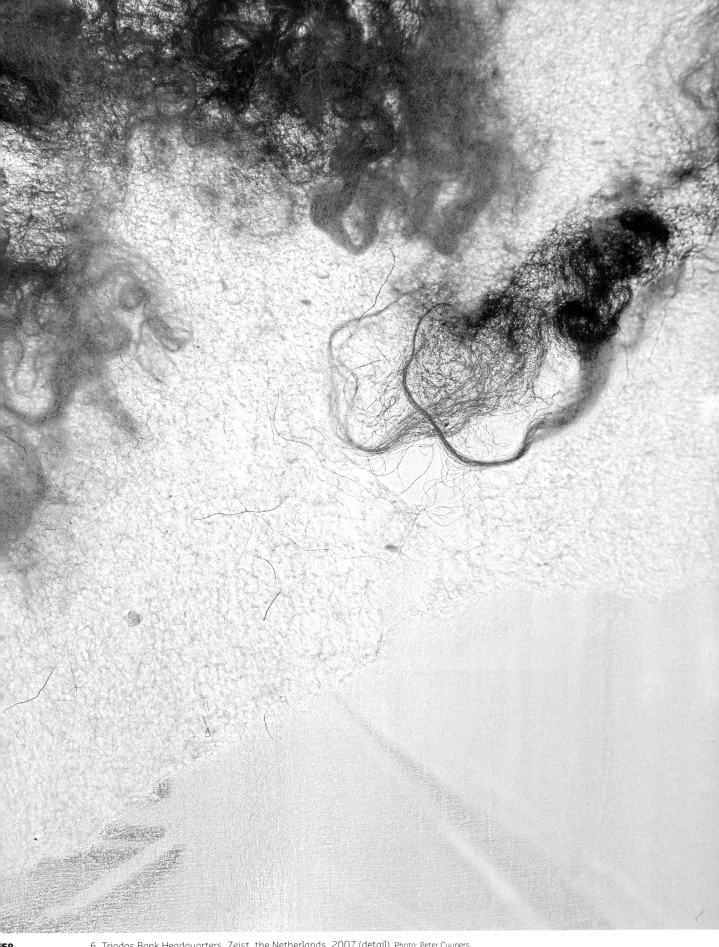

6. Triodos Bank Headquarters, Zeist, the Netherlands, 2007 (detail). Photo: Peter Cuypers

Beech

7. Triodos Bank Headquarters, Zeist, the Netherlands, 2007. Architect: Rau & Partners. Felt panels designed by Claudy Jongstra. Made by Studio Claudy Jongstra. Drenthe Heath, Wesleydale, and Merino wools, silk organza, raw silk. Photo: Peter Cuypers

In furniture design, textiles are typically relegated to a superficial role. As upholstery, textiles are secondary, interchangeable coverings for forms made from other materials—often environmentally harmful foams. A number of designers are experimenting with creating three-dimensional forms from solid, dense felt, which can be firm enough to provide support and structure while maintaining desirably soft surface qualities. Felt is isotropic, or uniform throughout, so it can be carved, literally. Danish designer Lene Frantzen's Slice is a cushion that has no cover and no stuffing; instead, colored wools are rolled and felted into a solid log, then cut in slices, revealing an interior that resembles the rings of a tree (fig. 8). Danish designer Pernelle Fagerlund, who describes her work as "textile furniture," has produced a number of seating pieces which have no structure other than the body and firmness of the textile components themselves. Her Textile Stones poufs are solid felt, covered with small balls cut in two, like geodes, to reveal their multicolored interiors (fig. 9).

8. The Slice. Designed and made by Lene Frantzen. Denmark, 2004. Wool, felted. Photo: Lene Frantzen

9. Textile Stones. Designed and made by Pernelle Fagerlund. Copenhagen, Denmark, 2008. Wool, felted.
Photo: Jeppe Gudmundsen-Holmgreen

Hairy Pottery, a collaboration between American designers Jorie Johnson and Clifton Monteith, represents an entirely unique functionality for felt. Johnson trained at the Rhode Island School of Design and has been working in Japan for nearly twenty years (fig. 10). Monteith is a furniture maker who traveled to Japan to study its traditional *urushi* lacquer technique. Lacquer does not dry like paint; rather, it cures in the presence of heat and moisture. Alternately, the curing can be effected through the addition of protein. Egg white, tofu, or rice paste is blended into the *urushiol* sap, and each gives a very different visual effect. When the two artists met, Johnson wondered why wool fibers, which are protein, could not be used as the curing agent. Years of experimentation led to the pair's conclusion that they can (figs. 11a, 11b).

Johnson and Monteith have made more than forty small vessels, but the first five took three and a half years.[3] Monteith turned a variety of bowl forms in his woodworking shop; Johnson formed her felt over these molds in a process very similar to hat making. *Kanshitu* lacquer is also done on a fabric substrate, but this is customarily a fine layer of cotton or hemp, so the use of a mold is required throughout the application of the many fine layers of lacquer. Once formed, the felt vessels are strong enough that no mold is required, yet flexible enough that Monteith can distort the forms slightly during the lacquering to give them a more organic quality. Fifty to seventy-five layers of lacquer are applied; sanding is done between applications to reexpose the chemically reactive sites on the protein fiber. The fuzz of wool fibers standing off the surface of the felt acts as a scaffold, giving the lacquer greater strength and integrity. Monteith calls the result "mother nature's fiberglass," or what that composite could be if the glass fibers were reactive with the resin, rather than inert.

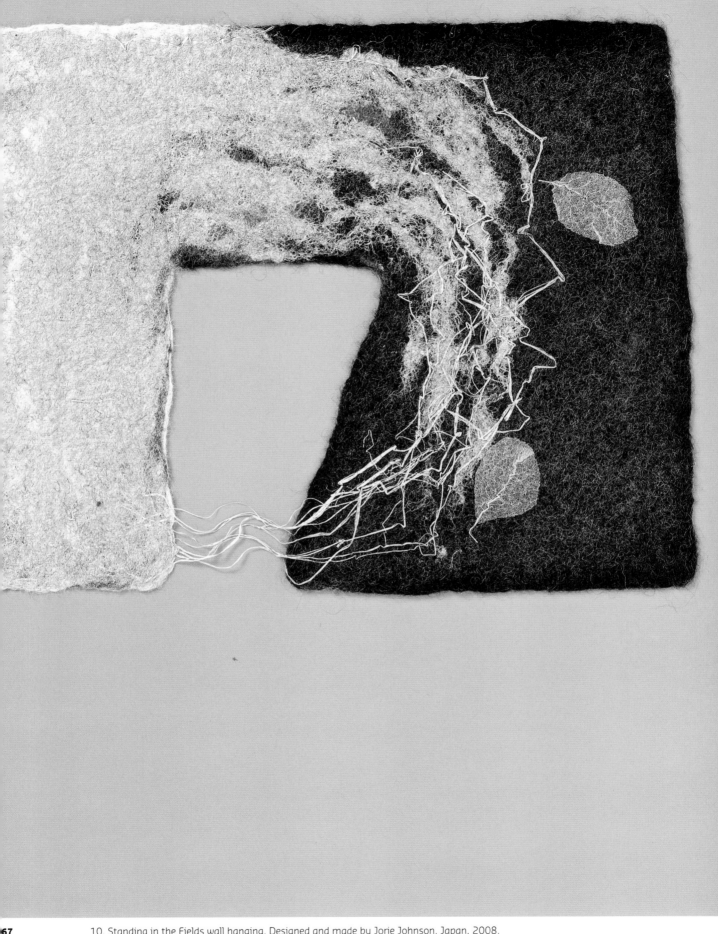

10. Standing in the Fields wall hanging. Designed and made by Jorie Johnson. Japan, 2008.
Wool, bast fiber, leaf. Photo: Yuzo Toyoda

11a. Winged Vessel II. Felt made by Jorie Johnson. Urushi lacquer by Clifton Monteith. Japan and United States, 2004. Wool, bast fibers, leaf, urushi lacquer. Photo: John Robert Williams

The range of materials encompassed by the term felt has expanded significantly over the past fifteen years—a period of intensive experimentation and innovation. The result is a lack of vocabulary suitable for describing the new techniques and processes. There is felt, of course, as both noun and verb. The term fulling is used to describe the final shrinking of the felted wool, but it also denotes the process of making woven or knitted wool textiles denser, like boiled wool. Other fibers lack the scaled composition of wool and will not felt, but they are sometimes added in small amounts for visual effect. Many felt makers refer to their "recipes": the exact proportions of each fiber type needed to achieve their desired effects. The concepts of dye-resist have been applied to controlled felting, using the resist medium to prevent the wool from shrinking in specific areas rather than resisting color. This is sometimes called *shibori* felting, for the traditional Japanese tie-dye method. Very dramatic textures have been created by preventing certain areas from shrinking, leaving islands of unfelted material in a densely felted ground. This technique is typically applied to woven or knitted textiles.

11b. Winged Vessel I. Felt made by Jorie Johnson. Urushi lacquer by Clifton Monteith. Japan and United States, 2004. Wool, bast fibers, leaf, urushi lacquer. Photo: John Robert Williams

12. Ursula Suter studio, Switzerland, 2008. Photos: Thomas Schirmann
a) Stitching plastic strips over the folded layer of fibers; b) The completed pleating and stitching

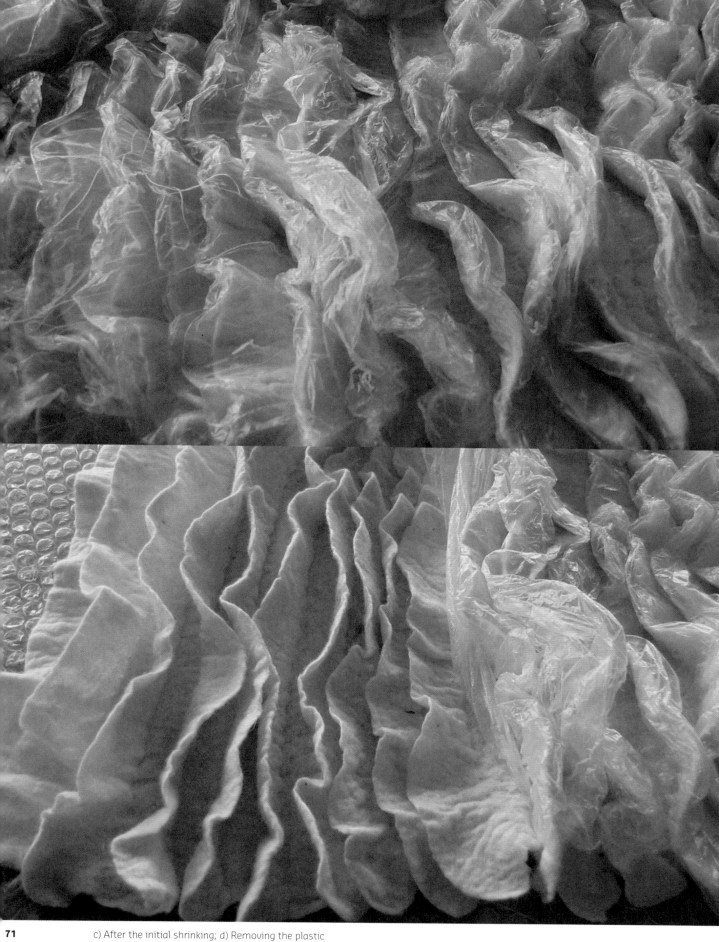

c) After the initial shrinking; d) Removing the plastic

Switzerland's Ursula Suter makes highly dimensional pieces employing this process within the parameters of true felting. Her technique is also closely related to forms of stitched-resist practiced in Japan and western Africa (figs. 12a–d). Suter begins with gossamer sheets of wool batting. With a needle and thread, she gently pleats, tucks, or ruches them in a series of parallel folds. Each fold is covered with a thin plastic strip and lightly stitched in place. When she proceeds to the wetting and agitation, no area is spared from shrinkage, but the raised area in the plastic strip felts only to itself, not to the background. When the felting is complete, the ridges stand off the surface in a variety of forms (figs. 13–15). In some cases, a cobweb-like layer of silk fibers is laid over the surface before felting, creating an effect similar to Persian lamb.

Nuno is the Japanese word for cloth, and nuno felting refers to the technique of felting through an existing fabric substrate. In the early 1990s, several artists, including Patricia Sparks and Polly Stirling, experimented with the concept. The term, coined by Stirling's assistant, Sachiko Kotaka, stuck. Attempting to create sheer, lightweight felts, they began using wool sparingly, coaxing the fibers through a sheer woven fabric, such as silk chiffon. They found that, if the weave was sufficiently open, the wool fibers would migrate through the woven fabric, creating a new type of material. This innovation had a major impact not only on felt making as a craft, but also on the uses for felt, as it allowed the creation of sheer textiles suitable for window treatments or soft, draping fabrics for fashion.

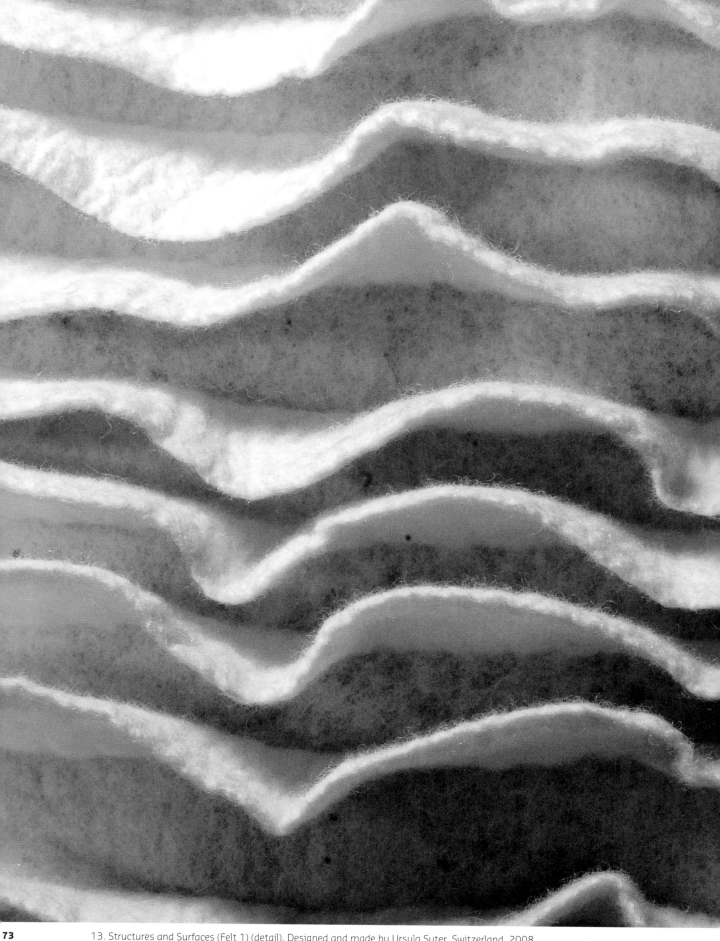

13. Structures and Surfaces (Felt 1) (detail). Designed and made by Ursula Suter. Switzerland, 2008.
Merino wool. Photo: Thomas Schirmann

14. Structures and Surfaces (Felts 1 and 2). Designed and made by Ursula Suter. Switzerland, 2008. Merino wool, silk. Photo: Thomas Schirmann

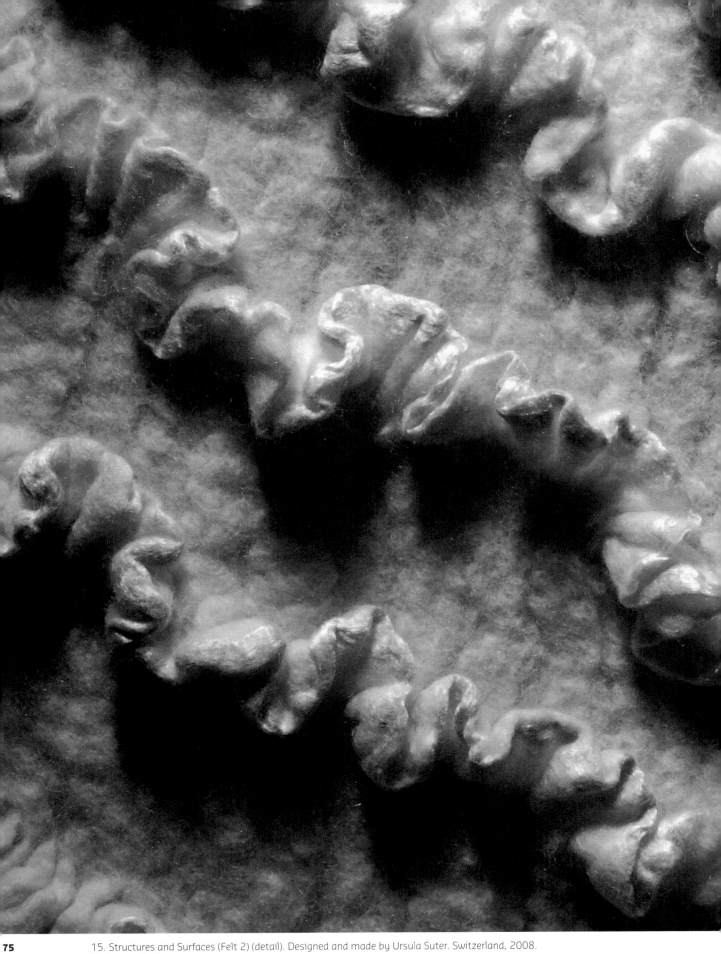

15. Structures and Surfaces (Felt 2) (detail). Designed and made by Ursula Suter. Switzerland, 2008.
Merino wool, silk. Photo: Thomas Schirmann

16a-d. (Clockwise from top left) Skirt and top, winter 2007; dress, summer 2008; skirt and top, summer 2008; dress, summer 2008. Designed by Christine Birkle. Manufactured by Hut Up. Germany. Wool, silk, cotton.
Photos: Christine Birkle

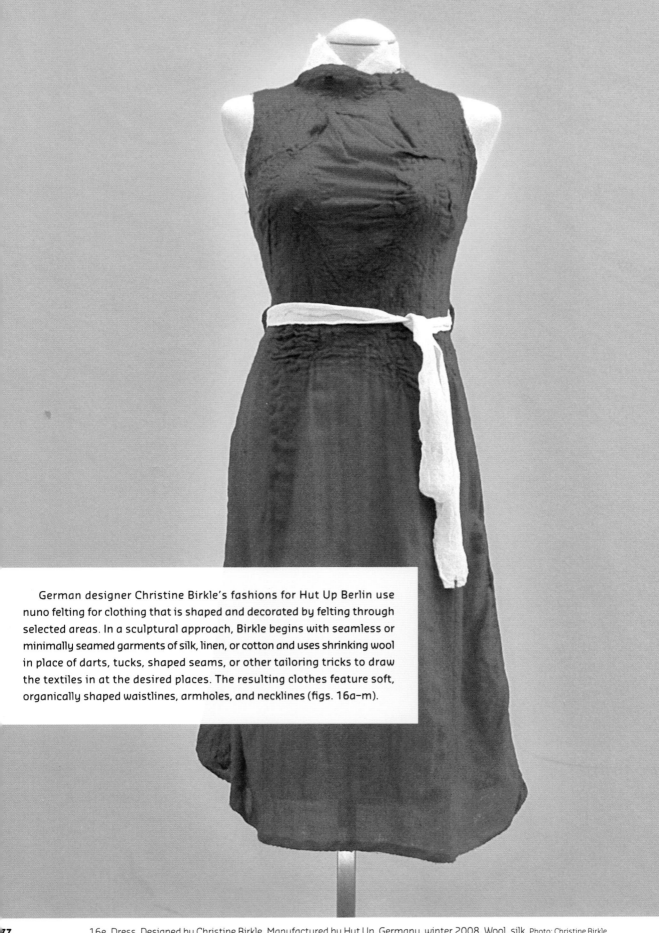

German designer Christine Birkle's fashions for Hut Up Berlin use nuno felting for clothing that is shaped and decorated by felting through selected areas. In a sculptural approach, Birkle begins with seamless or minimally seamed garments of silk, linen, or cotton and uses shrinking wool in place of darts, tucks, shaped seams, or other tailoring tricks to draw the textiles in at the desired places. The resulting clothes feature soft, organically shaped waistlines, armholes, and necklines (figs. 16a–m).

16e. Dress. Designed by Christine Birkle. Manufactured by Hut Up. Germany, winter 2008. Wool, silk. Photo: Christine Birkle

16f–i. (Clockwise from top left) Dress, summer 2008; jacket and skirt, winter 2007; dress, winter 2007; jacket, dress, and scarf, winter 2008. Designed by Christine Birkle. Manufactured by Hut Up. Germany. Wool, silk, cotton. Photos: Christine Birkle

16j–m. (Clockwise from top left) Dress; skirt and top; dress; skirt and top. Designed by Christine Birkle. Manufactured by Hut Up. Germany, winter 2007. Wool, silk, cotton, metallic fiber. Photos: Christine Birkle

Artists have developed a seemingly endless variety of "hybrid" felts incorporating different materials. All kinds of fabrics, including metallic organza, silk, and velvet, have been drawn into service as substrates for felting. As the wool begins to shrink and felt through the sheer areas, the velvet does not, but becomes crumpled and richly textured. Layers of silk can be laminated together, with wool used very sparingly as the glue. Lightly pre-felting sheets of wool can lead to more precise designs, as shapes can be cut from these sheets, rather than formed from loose fiber, in something like a felt appliqué or reverse appliqué. This is the technique used for Janice Arnold's Lumber Room project, a large-scale installation inside a community meeting space, arts center, and artist residency program in Portland, Oregon. The center, in its visual language, plays off the metaphor of the lumber room as storehouse of treasures or raw potential. Arnold is producing twenty-four felt panels, each twelve feet long, in a white-on-white pattern which evokes the cellular structure of wood (fig. 17). Since the lay-up is usually about forty percent larger than the finished piece, Arnold must work outdoors at her studio in Centralia, Washington. Large sheets are lightly pre-felted, and 5,000 to 6,000 individual holes are cut by hand in each panel. The lacy result is sandwiched between two layers of sheer silk and then felted again so that the wool fibers migrate out through the silk on both sides, forming a single textile. The elegant simplicity of the finished product belies the challenge of handling the cobweb-like sheets, which are over twenty feet long.

Despite its delicacy, this is a fairly straightforward recipe for Arnold. She often makes very complex lay-ups that may include six or seven different families of materials: silk fabrics, metallics, cut velvets, cotton or linen gauze; and wool, silk, and soy fibers. Jorie Johnson has used the term inlay to describe the method of using wool to hold together disparate elements, but the traditional, all-wool *ala kiiz* carpets of Central Asia are sometimes called inlay in English texts. The approach might more accurately be called collage or mixed media, except that, as with the lacquer, the components are not simply layered, but transformed into something new.

17. Lumber Room Art Sheers (series of 26). Window concept and design by Nicole Misiti, The Felt Hat.
Sheers designed by Janice Arnold. Made by JA FELT. Sponsored by Sarah Meigs. Portland, OR, 2008. Silk, wool.
Photo: Bob Iyalls

18. Dragonettes costume from Grendel. Composed by Elliot Goldenthal. Directed by Julie Taymor.
Produced by LA Opera. Costumes designed by Constance Hoffman. Felt fabrics designed and made
by Janice Arnold. Los Angeles, CA, 2006. Merino wool, silk, soy silk, metallic fiber.
Photo: Robert Millard/LA Opera

While these felts also have a support fabric, it is buried inside rather than on the outside. To call it a base fabric might be misleading, as Arnold might add layers to the front, back, or both. Inspired by natural phenomena, she creates textures which are complex and varied. In collaboration with costume designer Constance Hoffman, she created two dramatically different textiles for the opera *Grendel*, directed by Julie Taymor and produced by the Los Angeles Opera. One, the skin of the dragon, was inspired by molten lava (fig. 18); the other, a dress, was inspired by the cold depth of a glacier. Both costumes involved a color transformation from top to bottom, so each individual piece of felt had to be engineered to the pattern of the completed costume. The costumes featured a complex layering of sheer silk fabrics, wool fiber, silk fiber, soy, and metallic fabrics, forming a misty landscape (figs. 19a–b). The fibers were applied in wisps, because even though many are hand-dyed for the piece, and others are blended by carding different colors of dyed fiber together, a certain amount of color blending occurs during the felting process, like watercolor painting. Shrinking does not adequately describe what the wool fibers do. The creep, they move, they blend, softening lines and colors. They also lock these delicate compositions together, transforming them into sturdy fabrics.

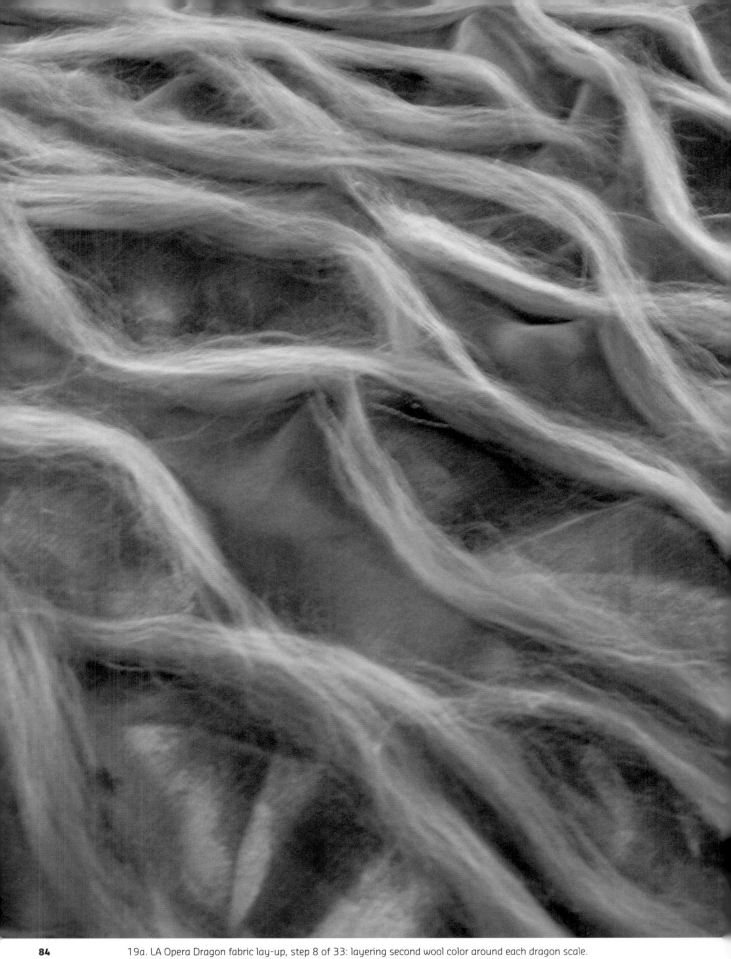

19a. LA Opera Dragon fabric lay-up, step 8 of 33: layering second wool color around each dragon scale.
JA FELT Studio, Centralia, WA, 2006. Photo: Janice Arnold

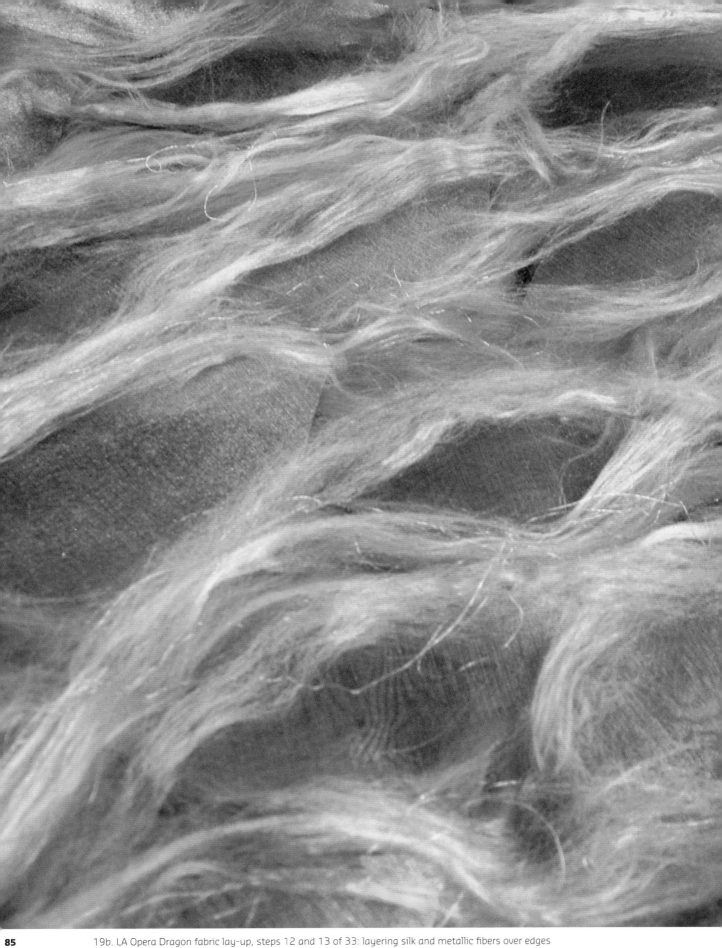

19b. LA Opera Dragon fabric lay-up, steps 12 and 13 of 33: layering silk and metallic fibers over edges of the 2nd dragon scale layer. JA FELT Studio, Centralia, WA, 2006. Photo: Janice Arnold

20a–d. Françoise Hoffmann studio, Lyon, France, 2008. Photos: David Desaleux
a) Hand-felting the sleeve with olive-oil soap and water; b) Rolling the garment in a reed mat;

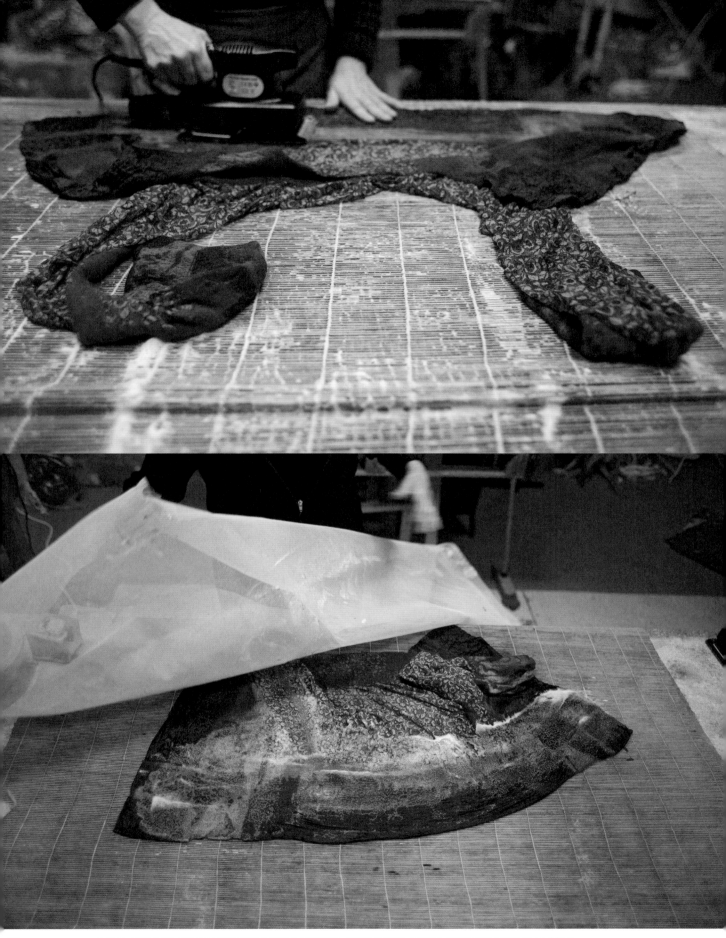

c) Spot-felting using the custom hand-felting machine; d) The wetted, soaped garment is ready to be felted

French felt maker Françoise Hoffmann also works in a collage style, but in three dimensions. Hoffmann is based in Lyon, and her fashions include many of the silk textiles for which the city is famous—silk velvets, lace, and other sumptuously feminine fabrics (fig. 21). Certain cultures rely on uncut cloth (think of the sarong or the sari); Western fashion has long prized fitted garments with complex piecing and seaming. The language of fashion so favors the tailored garment that the epitome of the craft is called *couture*: literally, sewing. Hoffmann says she is not sure the term can be applied to her *"travail de moulage"*—her practice of molding her seamless garments.

Hoffmann begins with a two-dimensional template, like a pattern, but it is cut from thick plastic sheeting, and its primary purpose is to prevent the front and back of her garment from felting to each other. She lays out a composition of silk fabrics, then overlays and connects them with carded tufts of colored merino wools. She gently wets the materials and begins to felt, either with her bare hands or with a small felting tool she has made from a palm sander (figs. 20a–d). Since she is forming the fabric and the garment simultaneously, she must anticipate many different interactions. For instance, the overall size and proportions of the garment will shrink relative to the template; since the wool is applied in a directional manner, it will shrink more in length than in width; the wool fibers will shrink, but the silk will not. Working from what will be the back side of the fabric, she must visualize the migration of the fibers to the front and the textural and color changes that will bring. In order to maintain the soft hand, the fibers must not be overworked. Needless to say, it is a very active process.

21. Roses. Designed and made by Françoise Hoffmann. Lyon, France, 2007. Wool, flocked tulle. Photo: Anna Solé

22. Ainay Graphique. Designed and made by Françoise Hoffmann. Lyon, France, 2007. Wool, silk. Photo: David Desaleux

A unique feature of Hoffmann's work is the incorporation of printed textiles—and the graphic aesthetic—into felt (fig. 22). She has the fabric, usually a sheer silk chiffon, digitally printed with a slightly enlarged version of what she envisions, anticipating that the text or image will become somewhat compressed during the felting process. While other felters have incorporated pictorial imagery into their works by laying in colored fibers, the effect tends to be primitive. Digital technology is one of the many tools Hoffmann brings to her feltmaking.

While many industrial designers today move easily among different media, textile designers tend to seek challenges within the discipline. In their felt-making practice, these designers have entered into discussions taking place across the design field: about new typologies, relationships among disciplines, flexibility and customization, sustainability, and the integration of digital tools with handcraft. In a world where we are bombarded with myriad, sometimes unreliable visual and auditory impressions, felt's materiality is perceived as authentic. The material's physicality and its cultural and historical associations resonate. There is a spiritual quality about engaging deeply with the physical world, and its effects can't be quantified, calculated, parsed. But it is a motivating force in design today, one that is making craft progressive again.

Custom technical felt components. Photo: Vereinigte Filzfabriken AG

FELT
TECHNOLOGY

Andrew Dent

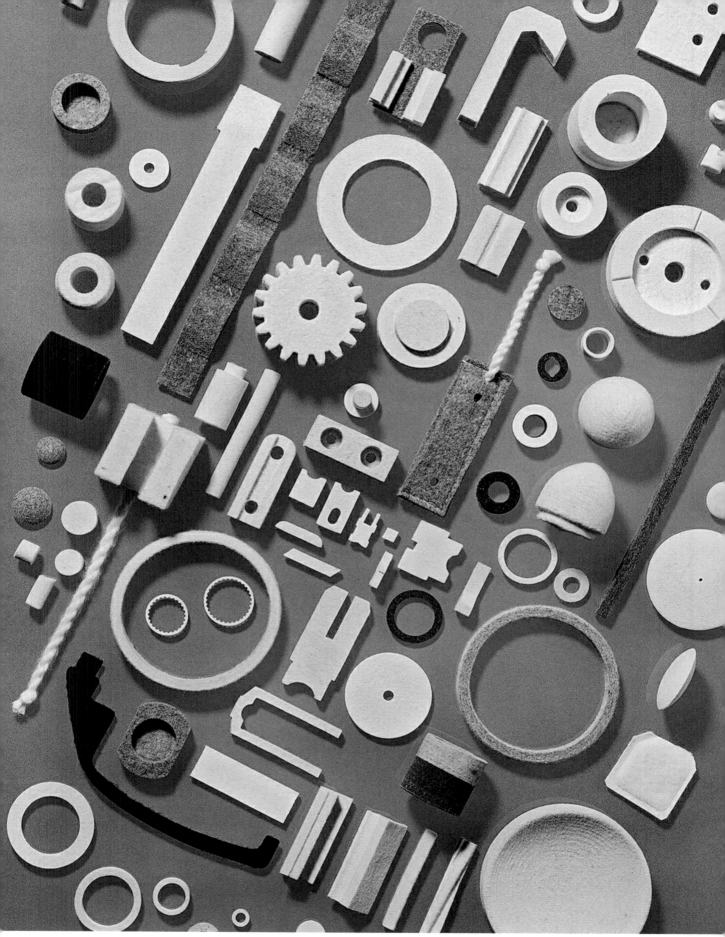

Custom technical felt components. Photo: Vereinigte Filzfabriken AG

Biomimetics is a relatively new discipline which acknowledges that nature has been developing materials and systems for millions of years, and posits that our often cumbersome solutions to problems can be greatly improved by looking to how plants and animals have solved similar issues. Though it is very much of the Zeitgeist in these times of concern over our industrial production methods, we have of course been learning and stealing from nature since we first picked up a tree branch, and this can be seen clearly in our approach to wool and one of its least lauded forms, felt.

Felt utilizes all of the natural advantages of raw wool fiber: durability, natural fire-retardance, UV stability, wicking and absorbing qualities, strength, retained flexibility after years of use, and an ability to accommodate processes such as cutting, sewing, nailing, laminating, and machining. It is not surprising that the highest-quality felt is unadulterated 100% wool fiber, produced in a similar method to the handmade versions of our early ancestors. Few products can equal its long history with so few changes to its original format. The fiber is hollow, and composed of α-keratin, the same protein-based material found in the hair, nails, hooves, and claws of mammals (this differs from β-keratin that makes up the claws, feathers, and beaks of birds and the scales and claws of reptiles). The physical properties of this hollow keratin fiber—flexibility, elasticity, a scaly outer structure, and often kinks in the strands—lend themselves to natural felting when rubbed together; and to very dense, strong, and rigid fabrics when this is done using industrial methods.

Felt is an essential material with a long list of applications, from home and automotive to industrial and aerospace, and it shows no sign of diminishing. Industrial felt, i.e., felt produced on an industrial scale for engineering and technical uses, is manufactured to a wide range of mechanical and physical specifications, depending upon the desired application. Felts generally have a service temperature from -80 to 200°F (this is the case for all wool materials). They have a maximum tensile strength below that of most plastics, but are still exceptionally strong for a material that contains no binders. They resist most acids and solvents but have a lower resistance to bases. They are highly compatible with oils and are used in many oil filtration and greasing applications.

1. Felt ovoid jacket and empire pants. Designed by Yeohlee Teng. United States, fall 2007. Wool.
Photo: William Palmer

The industrial felts discussed here are exclusively "wet processed" wool felts. The term felt is loosely applied to a wide range of non-woven synthetic materials, made from nylon, polyester, viscose, or even glass fiber, and produced by methods such as needle-punching or heat-bonding. Though these more modern, synthetic felts are interchangeable with wool felt in certain applications, none has the ubiquity and versatility of the all-natural original. The raw material comes, of course, from sheep, and the livestock's breed and origin are important to the quality of the wool. South Africa, Australia, New Zealand, and Texas are well-known suppliers of high-quality wool for felt; recently, India and other countries have started producing wool, but of insufficient quality for most engineering applications. For felts used in hats or clothing, softer wools such as Merino are used. Industrial felt has traditionally been eschewed for fashion because it is non-woven and has limited drape compared to woven and knit fabrics. However, its sculptural quality can sometimes be used to dramatic effect, as in this coat from Yeohlee Teng (fig. 1). These higher-quality wools are not regularly used for industrial applications due to their cost and their reduced mechanical properties.

The process for making roll and sheet felt has changed little since it was automated during the Industrial Revolution. Wool delivered from sheep farms contains contaminants such as burrs, twigs, and seeds that the animals have picked up in their fleece. Specialist cleaning and blending companies sort the wool by fineness and length of fiber, then wash or "scour" it to remove contaminants as well as the natural oil or lanolin from the surface of the wool fibers. It is then further cleaned by a process called "carbonizing," which burns away any residual plant matter. Care must be taken in this step not to shorten the length of the wool fiber or damage its scale structure, which would render the material suitable only for certain lower-grade felting.[1] Wool is mostly carbonized in the United States in order to ensure the uniformity of the resulting felt. Avoiding the process, as many Canadian and European manufacturers do, reduces the overall environmental impact of the manufacturing process. The cleaned wool is blown through to a large holding vat, which mixes the wool fibers together. For blended felts, other fibers such as rayon or viscose can be introduced at this time; however, the addition of non-wool fibers dramatically changes the felt's performance and is often viewed as diluting its quality. This is due to the lack of scales on synthetic fibers essential to interlocking during the felting process.

The blended wool is then placed into large carding machines, which draw the wool fiber out on large rotating combs and orient the fibers in one direction (fig. 2a). This step layers the fibers to produce a batt, or sheet of oriented fibers. Specialist carding machines can also cross-layer the batts—like the warp and weft of woven fabrics—to enhance the multidirectional strength of the sheet. Batts of fiber are bonded together on a fulling machine, which employs large metal plates to compress the fibers. Steam is forced between the plates to make the scales on the wool fiber swell, then the two plates oscillate in opposite directions, causing the wool fibers to rub together and their scales to interlock, and the felting process begins (fig. 2b). The longer the fabric remains between the hardening plates, the thinner, harder, and denser it becomes. This process determines the final width, roll length, and thickness produced, and is governed by specific formulations for each grade of felt. As the fibers interlock, they become shorter. This causes the width and length of the piece of felt to shrink. For most industrial and technical felts, the hardening stage produces a near-finished product which only requires drying. From initial carding to final felting, the process takes the best part of one day (fig. 2c).

For more technical felts of very high density, a more extreme process is required. The felt is bathed in an acid solution and then further rolled and pressed. This removes water from the wool and shrinks the fiber lengths, increasing their entanglement. Once the required density has been met, the felt is then bathed in base solution to neutralize any residual acid. The felt is now fully dense, but still contains water. There are two types of drying methods. Natural drying, though time-consuming, is thought to give the felt greater long-term stability, as the water is removed slowly, allowing the felt to relax and obtain a natural finish; its thickness and width should change only slightly as a result. A quicker but more expensive method is forced drying in gas-fired ovens. The felt is placed on a conveyor belt, and tenterhooks on either side penetrate the edge and effectively keep the material taut as it is dried (the holes made by the hooks can still be seen on the finished product). The felt is slowly pulled through the oven, and all the remaining moisture is forced from the fabric. It is believed that this places a residual tension in the material, which can cause problems when it is further manipulated into components, such as lifting or springing when cut, as the tension in the roll is released.

2. The manufacture of industrial felt. Photos: Verinigte Filzfabriken AG
a) Mixing the wool;

b) Forcing steam through the batts; c) Coming off the felting machine

The vast majority of industrial felt never requires coloring, as its function is performance, not aesthetics. They are typically off-white or mottled gray, with the color difference indicating the quality of the wool—off-white denotes a 100% virgin wool composition; gray suggests that lower-quality or recycled wool or perhaps non-wool fibers such as viscose or nylon have been blended in. The color consistency of these gray felts is rarely an issue, a fact that can sometimes be used to creative effect. The Joseph felt bench, a simple seat designed by Chris Ferebee and Laurice Parkin for 521 Design, is created by stacking a number of different shades of die-cut, non-virgin wool felts, contrasted by a single virgin layer in the middle (fig. 3). It is possible to color virgin wool felt—the gray can be colored, but really only to black—either in the wool prior to felting or after the sheet has been produced, either roll by roll or as a batch dyeing process for numerous rolls. Dyeing the roll limits the thickness of the sheet that may be colored, as it is difficult and time-consuming to get the dye to infiltrate to the center of the dense felt. Batch dyeing allows for greater consistency between rolls, but requires a greater inventory to be maintained, and is typically used only for more popular colors. Designers requiring a range of colors often need to obtain them from more than one supplier or have them custom-dyed, as the Dutch company Lama Concept did for the thirty-two shades of felt strip offered in its Cell carpet.

3. Joseph felt bench. Designed by Chris Ferebee and Laurice Parkin. Manufactured by 521 Design. Brooklyn, NY, 2000. Adhered, die-cut industrial wool felt. Photo: Nick Vaccaro Photography

4. Prince chair. Designed by Louise Campbell. Manufactured by Hay. Denmark, designed 2001, launched 2005.
Powder-coated steel, neoprene rubber, wool felt. Photo: Hay

Once manufactured, felt can be cut or shaped to clients' specifications. The material is cut using a blade, water, or, more recently, a laser, though laser cutting has a tendency to singe the wool fibers, especially with thicker felt sections. The traditional method is to cut with a blade, either a mechanical vibrating knife or a "band knife," similar to a bandsaw. Higher densities of felt can be cut on a lathe to create more complex forms and angled edges. The felt can be laminated, using a hot melt adhesive, onto various other materials, including chipboard, rubber, cork, or itself. An example of lamination, in this case onto a synthetic rubber called neoprene, is the Prince Chair by Louise Campbell (fig. 4), which she designed in 2001 for a competition to design a chair for Crown Prince Frederik of Denmark. The lace effect of the Prince Chair was created by a water jet cutting the laminated felt and rubber, which were in turn laminated to laser-cut steel. A similar process is used for Majken Mann's Spot carpets (fig. 5), which utilize a central laminated rubber core sheet. Different colors of felt sheet are used on the outer surfaces, with the complete sandwich construction cut with a water jet to create the outline and the "spots." The layering produces a highly cushioned sheet, offering a surface somewhat between a rug and a cushion.

5. Spot rug. Designed by Majken Mann and Nynne Faerch. Manufactured by Massimo. Copenhagen, Denmark, 2007. Wool felt, rubber. Photo: Bent Mann

As it is difficult to dye thick felt with any degree of accuracy, lamination is often the best way to achieve sharp differentiations in color. The Cell carpet, which features striking lines within a rug, shows this to great effect. Felted wool sheets of varying thicknesses are laminated together and cut into strips, which are then joined together using a polyester woven backing to create a flexible sheet. Small, eye-shaped nodes of wool felt are incorporated by randomly laying a felt string between the sheets before they are cut into strips, giving the impression of a cell structure (fig. 6). Damaged strips may be swapped out from the mat, allowing for easy repair. In a recent version called Cell LED, white LED lights are inserted into the carpet between the top surface and the backing. The LEDs, placed at the nodes, shine through the felt and create a diffuse glow (fig. 7); it looks just like the regular Cell carpet when the lights are off. Cell LED has been incorporated as safety floor lighting in the Airbus A350 Twinjet concept interior (fig. 8). LEDs, which require very little energy, produce no heat, and have a lifetime of approximately one hundred thousand hours, are ideal for this application.

6. Cell carpet strings. Designed by Yvonne Laurysen and Erik Mantel. Manufactured by LAMA Concept. The Netherlands, 2004. Wool felt. Photo: LAMA Concept

7. Cell LED carpet. Designed by Yvonne Laurysen and Erik Mantel. Manufactured by LAMA Concept.
The Netherlands, 2006. Wool felt, light-emitting diodes (LEDs). Photo: LAMA Concept

Grades of Felt

A relatively strict system of classification has been developed to allow users to choose the density, fiber content, and, as a result, physical and mechanical properties of felt within specific tolerances. For example, density, which determines major property differences, is measured in pounds per square yard: if a 36" x 36" x 1" felt sheet weighs 20 lbs., it is called 20-lb. felt. There are a number of classification systems, though the most widely used is the SAE (Society of Automotive Engineers) number. SAE numbers range from F1 to F26,[2] though additional grades up to F50 have been used to sub-classify some ranges. F1 denotes the highest density (16 lbs/yd² for 1" thick), the lowest liquid absorption, and the best mechanical properties, such as tensile strength, hardness, and resistance to compression and elongation. F26, the lowest density in this range, has half the density, double the liquid absorption, a factor-of-ten loss in tensile strength, and double the elongation. In general, the high-density grades (F1–F3 as well as F50) are used as washers and bushings, for polishing, and for applications where oil and grease are to be fed or retained. The mid-density felts (F5–F11) are used for dust shields, vibration mounts, and wipers. The low-density felts (F13–F26) are used for sound deadening, packing, padding, and other applications where mechanical properties such as abrasion and wear-resistance are not important.

8. Airbus A350 Twinjet concept. Designed by Airbus Design Team and Priestman Goode. Hamburg, Germany, and Toulouse, France, 2007. Rendering: Airbus

In addition, custom technical felts offer specified mechanical properties above and beyond the standard properties of the SAE felts.[3] These
include higher strengths and higher densities (up to 32 lbs./yd^2 for 1"
thick). Composed of 100% wool, technical felt sheets are stiff, almost
wood-like in weight and rigidity. They are suitable for machining with
metal tools to create custom shapes, and this type of forming is often
used for precision bearings and polishing wheels for large optical lenses
and jewelry. The stiffness of high-density felts allows them to transi-
tion into structural elements. Gaetano Pesce used this blurring of line
between structure and upholstery in his Feltri chair for Cassina (fig. 9),
made from a single sheet of industrial felt. Although the lower section of
the chair is impregnated with a polyester resin to maintain the curve of
the form, the back, also part of the same sheet, offers the user a degree
of support not usually possible in a textile.

9. Feltri chair. Designed by Gaetano Pesce. Manufactured by Cassina S.p.A. Italy, 1987.
Wool felt, polyester resin, hemp, cotton upholstery, polyester padding. Photo: Cassina

10a-b. Felt Rocks. Designed by Stephanie Forsythe and Todd MacAllen.
Produced by molo. Canada, 2005. Wool felt. Photo: molo

For an industrial material with such a wide range of properties, there are, not surprisingly, numerous industrial applications. Many of them came about initially because no alternative was available, but it is a tribute to felt's versatility that it remains the best or only solution in so many cases. For instance, felt is used for piano key hammers, and there are currently no viable synthetic alternatives. The hardness of a piano hammer influences greatly the resulting piano sound. Hard hammers are better at exciting high-frequency modes of a piano string's vibration, and the resulting tone quality can be described as bright or tinny. Soft hammers do not excite high frequencies very well, and the resulting tone is more dull or dark. In a typical piano, treble hammers are much harder than bass hammers.[4]

To produce very high density felts, an additional compacting process in a kicker or hammer mill is required to produce the desired density. Small clumps and chunks of felt are added as filler to improve the bite of the machine. Over time, they are pounded into highly dense, randomly shaped pieces resembling river rocks. These limited byproducts are cleaned, dyed, and sold by molo, in both natural and colored versions—a waste product reclaimed as a design object (fig. 10a). Dyeing the rocks achieves only a superficial coloring in the first fraction of an inch; the inner core remains impervious (fig. 10b).

While highly dense felt is effective for piano hammers and polishing wheels, lower-density felts are valuable where sound and vibration damping or thermal insulation is required, due to a need for interstices

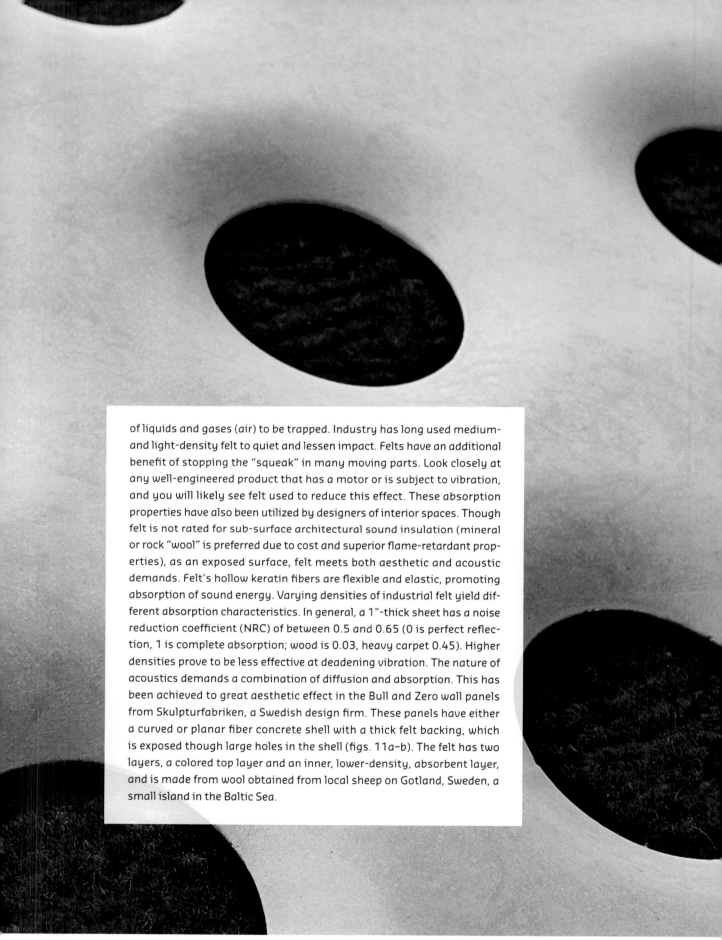

of liquids and gases (air) to be trapped. Industry has long used medium- and light-density felt to quiet and lessen impact. Felts have an additional benefit of stopping the "squeak" in many moving parts. Look closely at any well-engineered product that has a motor or is subject to vibration, and you will likely see felt used to reduce this effect. These absorption properties have also been utilized by designers of interior spaces. Though felt is not rated for sub-surface architectural sound insulation (mineral or rock "wool" is preferred due to cost and superior flame-retardant properties), as an exposed surface, felt meets both aesthetic and acoustic demands. Felt's hollow keratin fibers are flexible and elastic, promoting absorption of sound energy. Varying densities of industrial felt yield different absorption characteristics. In general, a 1"-thick sheet has a noise reduction coefficient (NRC) of between 0.5 and 0.65 (0 is perfect reflection, 1 is complete absorption; wood is 0.03, heavy carpet 0.45). Higher densities prove to be less effective at deadening vibration. The nature of acoustics demands a combination of diffusion and absorption. This has been achieved to great aesthetic effect in the Bull and Zero wall panels from Skulpturfabriken, a Swedish design firm. These panels have either a curved or planar fiber concrete shell with a thick felt backing, which is exposed though large holes in the shell (figs. 11a–b). The felt has two layers, a colored top layer and an inner, lower-density, absorbent layer, and is made from wool obtained from local sheep on Gotland, Sweden, a small island in the Baltic Sea.

11a. Bull acoustic tiles. Designed by Stina Lindholm. Manufactured by Skulpturfabriken. Sweden, 2004. Fiber concrete, wool felt. Photo: Stina Lindholm

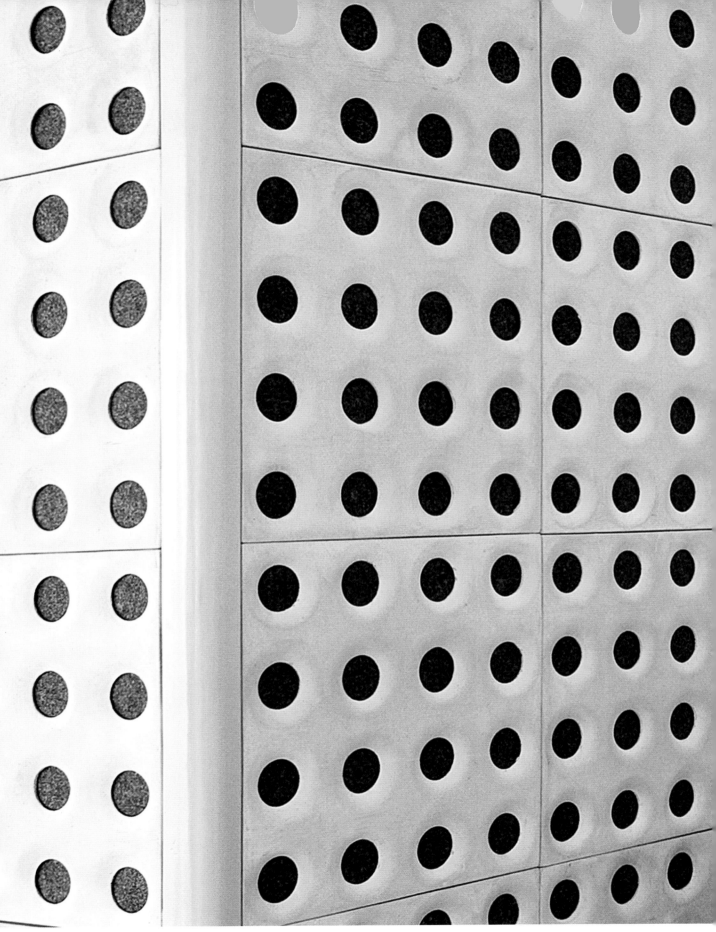

11b. Louis de Geer concert hall, Norrköping, Sweden, 2008. Architect: AG Architects/Per Wallgren.
Bull acoustic tiles by Skulpturfabriken. Fiber concrete, wool felt. Photo: Stina Lindholm

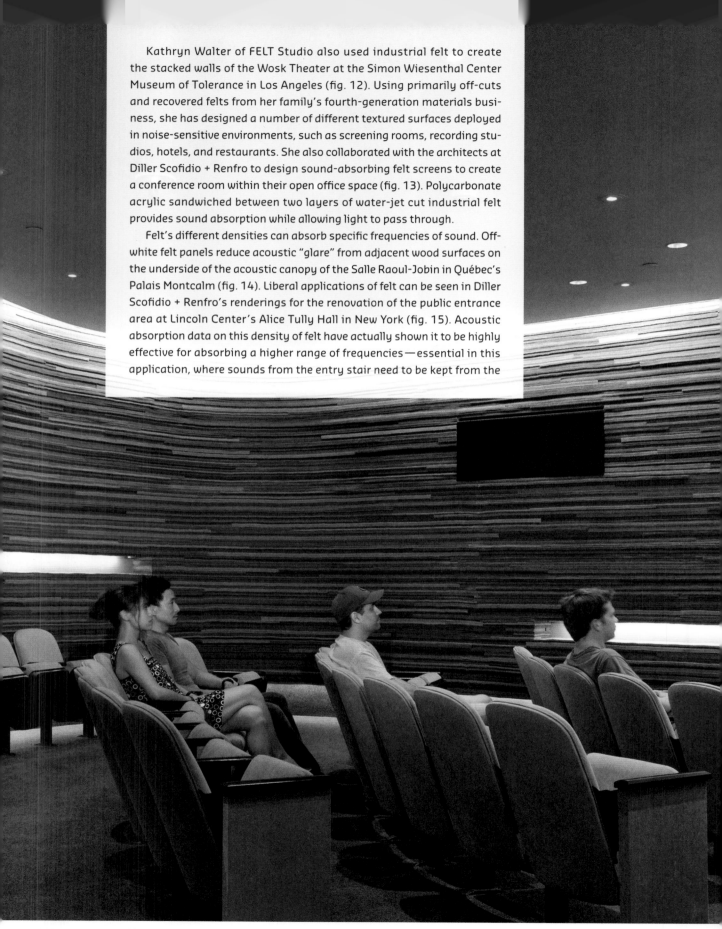

Kathryn Walter of FELT Studio also used industrial felt to create the stacked walls of the Wosk Theater at the Simon Wiesenthal Center Museum of Tolerance in Los Angeles (fig. 12). Using primarily off-cuts and recovered felts from her family's fourth-generation materials business, she has designed a number of different textured surfaces deployed in noise-sensitive environments, such as screening rooms, recording studios, hotels, and restaurants. She also collaborated with the architects at Diller Scofidio + Renfro to design sound-absorbing felt screens to create a conference room within their open office space (fig. 13). Polycarbonate acrylic sandwiched between two layers of water-jet cut industrial felt provides sound absorption while allowing light to pass through.

Felt's different densities can absorb specific frequencies of sound. Off-white felt panels reduce acoustic "glare" from adjacent wood surfaces on the underside of the acoustic canopy of the Salle Raoul-Jobin in Québec's Palais Montcalm (fig. 14). Liberal applications of felt can be seen in Diller Scofidio + Renfro's renderings for the renovation of the public entrance area at Lincoln Center's Alice Tully Hall in New York (fig. 15). Acoustic absorption data on this density of felt have actually shown it to be highly effective for absorbing a higher range of frequencies — essential in this application, where sounds from the entry stair need to be kept from the

12. Wosk Theater, Simon Wiesenthal Center Museum of Tolerance, Los Angeles, CA, 2007–08. Architect: Yazdani Studio of Cannon Design, Mehrdad Yazdani, Design Principal; Paul Gonzales, Project Manager; Jessica Yi, Project Architect; Hansol Park, AIA, Senior Designer; Jeremy Whitener, Project Designer. Felt walls designed and made by Kathryn Walter of FELT Studio. Industrial felts of wool and recycled fibers. Photo: Anne Garrison of Hewitt Garrison Photography

13. Felt wall panels for conference room of Diller Scofidio + Renfro. Designed by Diller Scofidio + Renfro. Fabricated by FELT Studio and E.F. Walter, Inc. New York, NY, 2006. Industrial wool felt, polycarbonate.
Photo: Donna Pallotta, © Diller Scofidio + Renfro

14. Acoustic canopy, Salle Raoul Jobin concert hall, Palais Montcalm, Québec City, Canada, 2007.
Architect: Jacques Plante, Consortium M.U.S.E. Acoustics consulting: Larry King, Jaffe Holden. Wool felt,
MDF panels, maple veneer, structural steel frame, aluminum vertical reflectors, integrated performance lighting.
Photo: Benoit LaFrance

15. Alice Tully Hall Main Entry Stairs, Lincoln Center, New York, NY, 2008. Architects: Diller Scofidio + Renfro/FxFowle.
Acoustic Consultant: Jaffe Holden. Graphic Design: 2x4. Felt consulting: Kathryn Walter/FELT Studio.
Installation: Turner Construction/Fine Construction. Wool felt wall and ceiling panels, LED-lit acrylic lettering.
Rendering: Diller Scofidio + Renfro/2x4

concert hall. Diller Scofidio + Renfro's handling of felt showcases a number of felt's unique characteristics. The felt will be applied in overlapping sheets so that its thick cut edge is revealed, creating a subtle decorative detail. The signage is water-jet-cut through the felt and back lit with LED lighting so that the monolithic surface is uninterrupted.

Felt was not considered suitable for the flooring in this heavily trafficked public venue, but the simplicity of felt flooring continues to appeal. Swiss carpet producer Ruckstuhl produces Feltro-Legno, a flooring in which matte wool felt is complemented by slats of polished oak—combining the noise-muffling effect of a thick carpet with the light-reflecting glow of hardwood (fig. 16). If a more shag effect is preferred, felt can be loomed into a pile carpet, as seen in Tord Boontje's Little Field of Flowers rug for Nanimarquina (fig. 17). Thin colored felt is die-cut into six different flower and leaf shapes and woven into the wool carpet, creating the effect of walking through a meadow.

Felt's ability to be cut without fraying is one of its most unique and compelling properties. Water-jet-cutting and die-cutting have been used to great effect, but cutting into felt has additional purposes other than simple decoration. Jean Nouvel's SKiN sofa for Molteni is essentially a one-piece felt sheet draped over a tubular, pre-tensioned steel frame; cutting the felt at specific points creates a seating surface with a scooped

16. Feltro-Legno carpet, Hotel Krafft, Basel, Switzerland, 2007. Designed and manufactured by Ruckstuhl AG. Wool felt, oak, polyurethane. Photo: Bruno Augsburger

17. Little Field of Flowers carpet. Designed by Studio Tord Boontje. Manufactured by Nanimarquina. Spain, 2006. Wool felt. Photo: Albert Font

18a. Skin sofa. Designed by Jean Nouvel. Manufactured by Molteni & C. Italy, 2008.
Wool felt, stainless steel. Photo: Tiziano Sartorio

18b. Skin sofa (detail). Photo: Tiziano Sartorio

19. Relief chair. Designed by Ben K. Mickus. Felt manufactured by Sutherland Felt. Felt cutting by Fab-Rite. Metal finishing by Evan Eisman Co. United States, 2008. Wool felt, stainless steel. Photo: Robert Bean

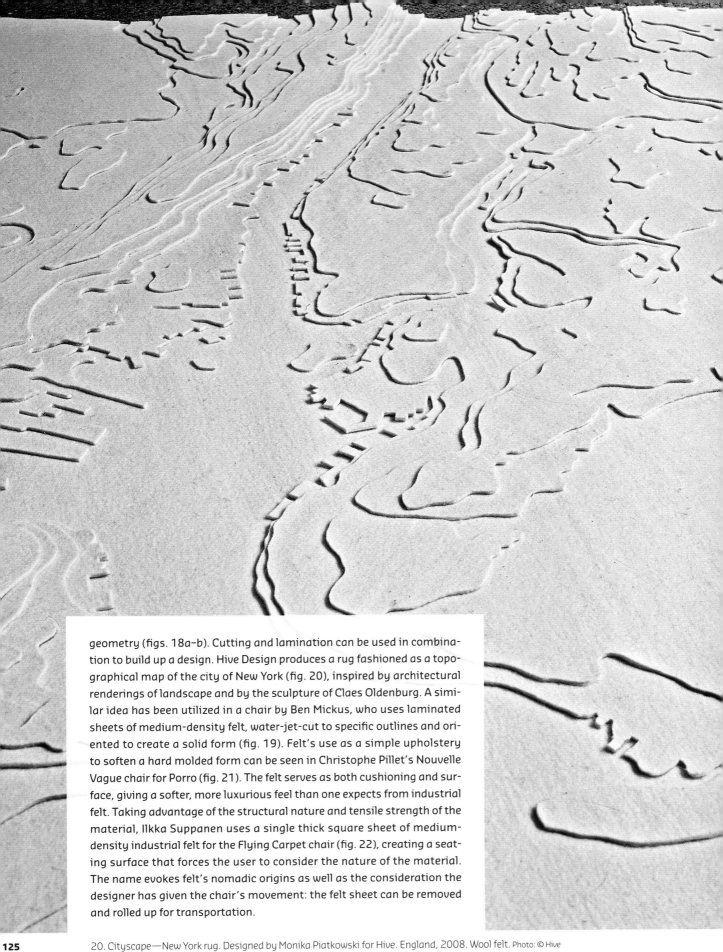

geometry (figs. 18a–b). Cutting and lamination can be used in combination to build up a design. Hive Design produces a rug fashioned as a topographical map of the city of New York (fig. 20), inspired by architectural renderings of landscape and by the sculpture of Claes Oldenburg. A similar idea has been utilized in a chair by Ben Mickus, who uses laminated sheets of medium-density felt, water-jet-cut to specific outlines and oriented to create a solid form (fig. 19). Felt's use as a simple upholstery to soften a hard molded form can be seen in Christophe Pillet's Nouvelle Vague chair for Porro (fig. 21). The felt serves as both cushioning and surface, giving a softer, more luxurious feel than one expects from industrial felt. Taking advantage of the structural nature and tensile strength of the material, Ilkka Suppanen uses a single thick square sheet of medium-density industrial felt for the Flying Carpet chair (fig. 22), creating a seating surface that forces the user to consider the nature of the material. The name evokes felt's nomadic origins as well as the consideration the designer has given the chair's movement: the felt sheet can be removed and rolled up for transportation.

20. Cityscape—New York rug. Designed by Monika Piatkowski for Hive. England, 2008. Wool felt. Photo: © Hive

21. Nouvelle Vague chair. Designed by Christophe Pillet. Manufactured by Porro srl. Italy, 2005.
Thermoplastic, wool felt. Photo: Tommaso Sartori

Industrial Felt and Sustainability

In this first part of the twenty-first century, environmental impact is of foremost consideration in any discussion of a material. Assessing sustainability has become more complex, as it involves not only the raw materials and processes to make a product, but its entire lifecycle once it is made and used. With textiles, it is often the processes used to clean, color, and finish the fabric, rather than its fiber composition, which constitute its greatest impact on the environment. The chemicals used to bleach and dye fabrics as well as flame-retardants, UV stabilizers, and anti-soiling treatments are all more likely to cause harm to the environment than the fiber, whether synthetic or natural. One of the major advantages of industrially produced, 100% wool felt is that there is little, if anything, added to the material, either during processing or for its myriad applications. No binders, stabilizers, or plasticizers are added to the fibers; and though chemicals are used to clean wool prior to felting, the vast majority of industrial felts are undyed and utilize no chemical post-treatment of the surface. Overall considerations of industrial wool felt suggest that this material has some advantageous sustainable considerations. Life Cycle Assessment (LCA) studies by New Zealand's Merino wool industry have shown that the total energy use and carbon-dioxide emissions for wool are lower than for comparable synthetic fibers; for example, nylon demands over 500% more energy; acrylic 380% more energy; and polyester 270% more energy to produce than wool fiber.[5] The LCA report does not consider the amount of methane sent into the atmosphere by the sheep—more than half of New Zealand's greenhouse-gas emissions come from its 45 million sheep—so exact comparisons are always going to be tough. In addition, the study does not incorporate information on the effects of the use and disposal of wool felt. An alternative approach to assessing environmental impact, known as "cradle to cradle," considers the entire cycle of the product, with the intention of putting the material back into the production loop—rather than "cradle to grave," in which the product ends up in a landfill. For industrial felt,

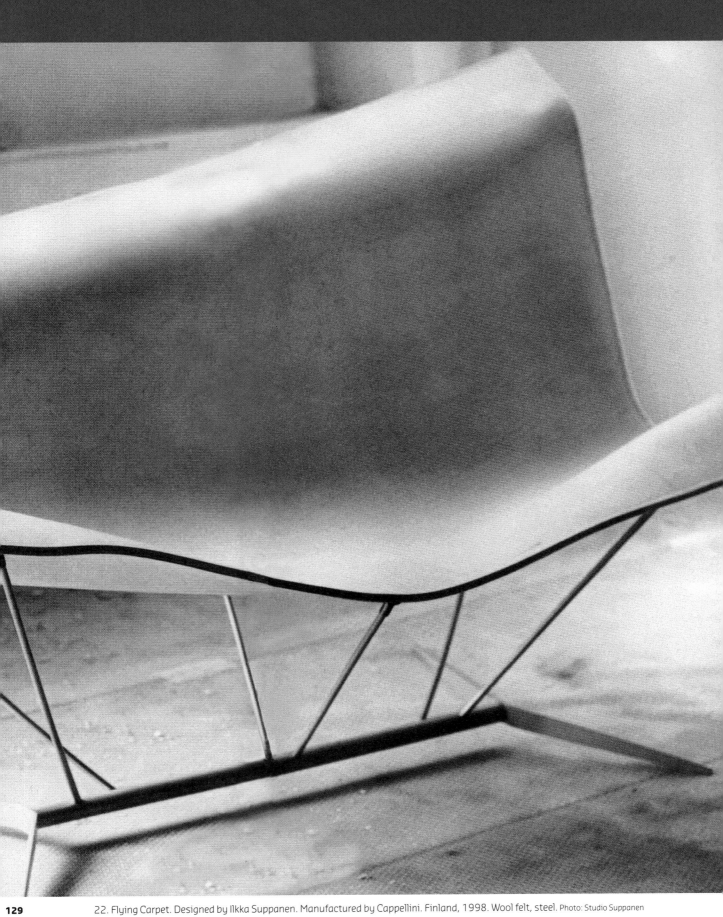

22. Flying Carpet. Designed by Ilkka Suppanen. Manufactured by Cappellini. Finland, 1998. Wool felt, steel. Photo: Studio Suppanen

Striations wall panel (detail). Designed and made by Kathryn Walter/FELT Studio. Toronto, Canada, 2007. Industrial felt of wool and recycled fibers. Photo: Kathryn Walter

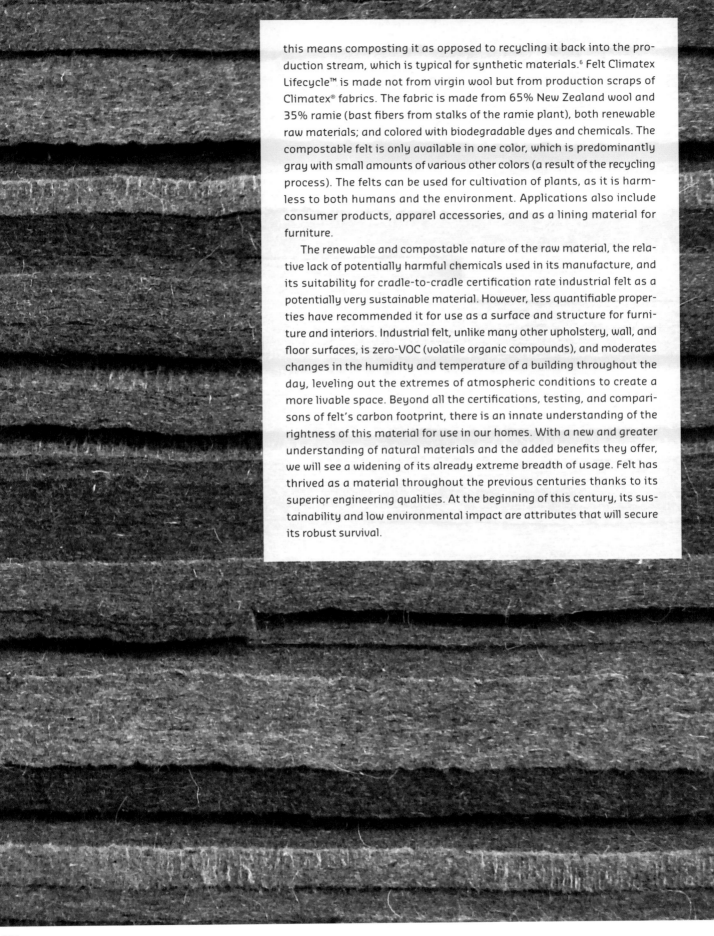

this means composting it as opposed to recycling it back into the production stream, which is typical for synthetic materials.[6] Felt Climatex Lifecycle™ is made not from virgin wool but from production scraps of Climatex® fabrics. The fabric is made from 65% New Zealand wool and 35% ramie (bast fibers from stalks of the ramie plant), both renewable raw materials; and colored with biodegradable dyes and chemicals. The compostable felt is only available in one color, which is predominantly gray with small amounts of various other colors (a result of the recycling process). The felts can be used for cultivation of plants, as it is harmless to both humans and the environment. Applications also include consumer products, apparel accessories, and as a lining material for furniture.

The renewable and compostable nature of the raw material, the relative lack of potentially harmful chemicals used in its manufacture, and its suitability for cradle-to-cradle certification rate industrial felt as a potentially very sustainable material. However, less quantifiable properties have recommended it for use as a surface and structure for furniture and interiors. Industrial felt, unlike many other upholstery, wall, and floor surfaces, is zero-VOC (volatile organic compounds), and moderates changes in the humidity and temperature of a building throughout the day, leveling out the extremes of atmospheric conditions to create a more livable space. Beyond all the certifications, testing, and comparisons of felt's carbon footprint, there is an innate understanding of the rightness of this material for use in our homes. With a new and greater understanding of natural materials and the added benefits they offer, we will see a widening of its already extreme breadth of usage. Felt has thrived as a material throughout the previous centuries thanks to its superior engineering qualities. At the beginning of this century, its sustainability and low environmental impact are attributes that will secure its robust survival.

Notes

Christine Martens

1   S.I. Rudenko, *The Frozen Tombs of Siberia: The Pazyryk Burials of Iron Age Horsemen* (London: J. M. Dent and Sons, 1970): 202.

2   V. M. Basilov, ed., *Nomads of Eurasia* (Seattle and London: University of Washington Press, 1989): 3.

3   B. Laufer, "The Early History of Felt," in *American Anthropologist*, New Series, vol. 32, Jan–March, no. 1, 1930: 1–18.

4   P. A. Andrews, *Felt Tents and Pavilions: The Nomadic Tradition and Its Interaction with Princely Tentage* (London: Melisande, 1999): 297. Originally published in I. de Rachewiltz, *The Secret History of the Mongols: A Mongolian Epic Chronicle of the Thirteenth Century* (Leiden: Brill, 1971–85), section 124.

5   M. E. Burkett, *The Art of the Feltmaker* (Kendall: Abbot Hall Art Gallery, 1979): 21.

6   Laufer, p. 15.

7   L. Batchuluun, *Felt Art of the Mongols* (Ulaanbaatar, Mongolia: Institute for the Study of Arts and Culture, Mongolian University of Arts and Culture, 2003): 33.

8   O. A. Gundogdiyev, "The Medieval Social and Military Structure of the Turkmans," in *Miras, Heritage Popular Scientific Journal* (Ashgabat, Turkmenistan, 2007): 80–85.

9   D. Tyson, "Shrine Pilgrimage in Turkmenistan as a Means to Understanding the Turkmen," in *Central Asian Monitor* online supplement, www.chalidze.com, no. 1, 1997.

10 C. Martens, "Lords of the Dance," in *HALI: Carpet, Textile and Islamic Art* 135 (London, 2004): 110–15.

11 H. Fathi, "The Otines, the Unknown Women Muslim Clerics of Central Asian Islam," in *Central Asian Survey*, vol. 16, no. 1 (March 1997): 27–43.

12 See Tyson.

13 Feltmaking continues today in regions of southern Uzbekistan, where the material is used in Boyson to line the trucks carrying fruits and vegetables to market.

14 *Atlas of Central Asian Artistic Crafts and Trades, vol. III: Kyrgyzstan* (Samarkand, Uzbekistan: International Institute for Central Asian Studies, 2002): 75.

15 Many felt designs have been influenced by a book published in the 1980s by Sadybakas Kadyraliev entitled *Uzory Sadybakas (Patterns of Sadybakas)*, which was received enthusiastically throughout Kyrgyzstan. As a result, many women choose patterns arbitrarily rather than looking to family or village traditions.

16 Conversation between the author and feltmakers in Kolkhoz Niazov, Mary Region, Turkmenistan, March 2008.

17 S. Demidov, *Tourism and Development*, no. 1 (Ashgabat, Turkmenistan, 1996): 42, 43.

18 Literally translated as "central hearth."

19 For this reason, camel hair can never be used for anything that touches the ground, such as socks or ordinary carpets.

20 Conversation between the author and N. Atasoy, 2006.

21 E. Celebi, *The Travel Writings of Evliya Celebi*, manuscript, 4/229a. Celebi's travel accounts are in ten volumes; there are copies in various libraries, but scholars do not know which are the originals. A ten-volume publication has been made of the best copies.

22 Ibid., 2/282a.

23 Ibid., 2/286b.

24 Ibid., 2/230b.

25 E. Celebi, *Evliya Celebi Seyahatnamesi*, transcribed by Seyit Ali Kahraman-Yucel Dagli (Istanbul: Yapi Kredi publications, Istanbul, 2003): 397.

26 Ibid., p. 599. Ebu Said-Tari, the patron saint of feltmakers and their guilds, was martyred together with Imam Huseyin. Feltmakers were known to make pilgrimages to his tomb in Karbala, where they would take an oath on his tomb.

27 Ibid.

28 Michael and Veronika Gervers, "Feltmaking Craftsmen of the Anatolian and Iranian Plateaux," in *Textile Museum Journal* I (Washington, D.C., 1974): 15–29.

29 Conversation between the author and Mehmet Girgic, 2001.

30 The *Surname* manuscript is in the Topkapi Palace Museum Library, Istanbul (H.1344). The text is also found in N. Atasoy, *Surname-i-Humayun, an Imperial Celebration* (Istanbul, 1997).

31 Batchuluun, p. 38.

32 Ibid., p. 58.

33 Ibid. p. 35.

34 Andrews, p. 287.

35 Ibid.

36 Ibid., p. 71.

37 Ibid., p. 73.

38 Ibid., p. 95.

39 Ibid., p. 103.

40 Ibid., p. 10.

Susan Brown

1   Kenneth Hayes, "Felt's Alterity," in Kathryn Walter, ed., *Felt* (Toronto: The Museum for Textiles, 2000): 6.
2   Andrea Zittel, "A Brief History of A–Z Uniforms," in text for the *A–Z Uniforms 1991–2002* exhibition, Andrea Rosen Gallery, New York, January 22–February 21, 2004.
3   Interview between the author and Clifton Monteith, April 23, 2008.

Andrew Dent

1   In the United States, carbonized wools are preferred, especially for white felts, as the resulting product is more uniform in accordance with Society of Automotive Engineers (SAE) standards. The SAE is a nonprofit, membership-based organization that generates and assesses standards for engineering methods and materials. Carbonizing is not essential; many European and Canadian felt manufacturers use scoured wool, depending on the application.
2   The F1 grade is equivalent to 16R1 in the Commercial Standard Grade system and 34R1 in the NTA numbering system. This is an old technology, with competing classifications used in different regions and industries.
3   The two terms "industrial" and "technical" are often interchangeable; in particular, German manufacturers call felts for specific engineering applications "technical."
4   Daniel A. Russell, Science and Mathematics department, GMI Engineering & Management Institute, 1997. "The Piano Hammer at a Nonlinear Spring," published on the Kettering University Web site, www.kettering.edu.
5   Andrew Barber and Glenys Pellow, *Life Cycle Assessment: New Zealand Merino Industry Merino Wool Total Energy Use and Carbon Dioxide Emissions* (Pukekohe, Auckland: The AgriBusiness Group, 2006).
6   There has also been an increase in the use of post-industrial recycled felts for various consumer products, such as bags, bowls, carpet underlay, and furniture lining. However, these are almost exclusively produced through needle-punching rather than wet-processing, excluding them from our current area of investigation.

Bibliography

Aimone, Katherine Duncan. "Jorie Johnson: Coaxing Fashion from Felt." In *Fiberarts* 28, no. 5 (March/April 2002): 30–33.

American Felt Company. *The Story of Felt.* Glenville, CT: American Felt Company, 1946.

Andrews, Peter A. *Felt Tents and Pavillions: The Nomadic Tradition and Its Interaction with Princely Tentage.* London: Melisende, 1999.

——. "Felt Tents in Anatolia." In *Sosyal Anthropoloji ve Etnoloji Dergisi* 4 (1986): 33–63.

——. "The White House of Khurasan: The Felt Tents of the Iranian Yomut and Göklen." In *Journal of Persian Studies* 9 (1973): 93–110.

Barber, E. J. W. *Prehistoric Textiles: The Development of Cloth in the Neolithic and Bronze Age.* Princeton: Princeton University Press, 1991.

Barkova, Ludmila. "The Pazyryk Felts." In *HALI*, no. 113 (November/December 2000): 74–79, 100.

Basilov, Vladimir N., and O. B. Naumova. "Yurts, Rugs and Felts." In *Nomads of Eurasia* (Seattle: University of Washington Press, 1989): 126–135.

Batchuluun, Luntengiin. *Felt Art of the Mongols,* trans. Eric Thrift. Ulaanbaatar: Institute for the Study of Arts and Culture; Mongolian University of Arts and Culture, 2003.

Beresneva, L. G. "Rugs and Felts of the Kasakh, Kirgiz, and Karakalpak People." In *Arts & the Islamic World*, no. 33 (August 1998): 80–84.

Bunn, Stephanie. "Diaries from Kyrgystan." In *Echoes, the Journal of the International Feltmaker's Association* 42 (1996): 26–31.

——. "Kazakh Quest." In *HALI*, no. 133 (March/April 2004): 17–19.

——. "Kirghiz Felt Carpets." In *HALI*, no. 93 (July 1997): 84–89.

——. "Kyrgyz Shyrdak." In *The Textile Museum Journal* 3445 (1995–96): 75–91.

——. "Mobile and Flexible Vernacular Dwellings." In Mathias Schwartz-Clauss, ed., *Living in Motion: Design and Architecture for Flexible Dwelling* (Weil am Rhein: Vitra Design Stuftung GmbH, 2002): 133–57.

——. "Patterns of Change." In *Crafts*, no. 147 (July/August 1997): 30–33.

Burkett, M. E. *The Art of the Felt Maker.* Kendall: Abbott Hall Gallery, 1970.

——. "An Early Date for the Origin of Felt." In *Anatolian Studies* 27 (1977): 111–15.

——. "Some New Aspects in the Study of the History of Felt Making." In *Oriental Carpet and Textile Studies IV.* Berkeley: San Francisco Bay Area Rug Society, 1993.

Chambros, Krystyna. "Quilted Ornamentation on Mongol Felts." In *Central Asiatic Journal* 32 (1986): 34–60.

Chen, Aric. "For the Love of Felt." In *Interior Design* 73, no. 11 (November 2002): 150–55.

Damgaard, Annette. *Filt: kunst teknik, historie.* Denmark: Forlaget Hoveland, 1994.

Douglas, William O. "Journey to Outer Mongolia." In *National Geographic* (March 1962): 289–345.

Dupaigne, B. "Aperçus sur quelques techniques afghanes." In *Objets et Mondes* 7, no. 1: 41–84.

Eiland, Murray Lee III. "Felting Between East and West." In *Visual Anthropology* 20, no. 4 (2007): 263–83.

Els-Dubelaar, Ria van. *Dutch Felt = Vilt in Beeld.* Franeker: Zijdar, 2005.

Faegre, Torvald. *Tents: Architecture of the Nomads.* New York: Doubleday, 1979.

Felt Facts: The Story of an Essential Material for Both Civilian and War Use. New York: The Felt Association, 1943.

A Felt Handbook: The Story of the Manufacture and Uses of Felts. Boston: The Felters Company, Inc., 1941.

Felting: An Exhibition of Traditional and Contemporary Work, exh. cat. New York: The American Craft Museum, 1980.

Gervers, Michael. "Evidence for Ottoman Influence on Felt-making in Egypt." In *Textile History* 20, no. 1 (1989): 3–12.

——. "Felt-making Craftsmen of the Anatolian Plateaux." In *The Textile Museum Journal* 4, no. 1 (December 1974): 14–29.

Gervers, Veronika. "Felt in Eurasia." In Anthony N. Landreau, ed., *Yoruk, the Nomadic Weaving Tradition of the Middle East* (Pittsburgh: Carnegie Institute, 1978): 16–22, 65–68.

——. "Felt-making Craftsmen of the Anatolian and Iranian Plateaux." In *Textile Museum Journal* 1 (1974): 15–29.

——. "Methods of Traditional Felt-making in Anatolia and Iran." In *Bulletin de Liaison du Centre International d'Étude des Textiles Anciens* 2, no. 38 (1973): 152–62.

——. "The Vanishing Cloaks of Afyon: Textile Treasures from Turkey and the Balkans." In *Rotunda* 6, no. 3 (1973): 4–15.

Gordon, Beverly. *Feltmaking: Traditions, Techniques, and Contemporary Explorations.* New York: Watson-Guptill Publications, 1980.

———. "Shelters and Symbols." In *Shuttle, Spindle & Dyepot* 2, no. 1: 53–62.

Gulacsi, Zsuzsanna. "Asian Felts, the Hand of Mani: Felt Rugs in Manichaean Miniatures." In *HALI*, no. 16 (June/July 1994): 80–85.

Heimstadt, Leslie. "Felt: How a Secret Spread." In *Shuttle, Spindle & Dyepot* 11, no. 1 (Winter 1979): 47–52.

Hirsch, Udo. "Capturing the Moment: Anatolian Felts." In *HALI*, no. 130 (September/October 2003), 84–85.

Johnson, Jorie. *Feltmaking and Wool Magic*. Gloucester, MA: Quarry Books, 2006.

Kuspit, Donald B. "Beuys: Fat, Felt and Alchemy." In *Art in America* 68 (May 1980): 78–89.

Lang, Marlène, ed. *Filzkunst: Tradition und Experiment*. Bern: Haupt, 2001.

Lang, Marlène, and Fabia Denninger. *Wohnen mit Filz: Projekte und Designideen*. Bern: Haupt, 2005.

Laufer, Berthold. "The Early History of Felt." In *American Anthropologist* 31, no. 1 (January–March 1930): 1–18.

Lauwen, Toon, ed. *Claudy Jongstra: Matter and Meaning*. Amsterdam: Artimo, 2005.

Levine, Louis D. "Notes on Felt-Making and the Production of Other Textiles at Seh Gabi, a Kurdish Village." In Veronika Gervers, ed., *Studies in Textile History* (Toronto: Royal Ontario Museum, 1977): 202–11.

MacDougal, Marleah. "Feltmaking in India: A Remnant of the Past." In *Fiberarts* 6 (November/December 1979): 10.

Martens, Christine. "The Felt Carpets of a Master Craftsman." In *HALI*, no. 120 (January/February 2002): 135–39.

———. "Lords of the Dance: The Dervish Sikke." In *HALI*, no. 135 (July/August 2004, supplemental special ed.): 110–15.

Mattera, Joanne. "Why Wool Felts." In *Fiberarts* 6 (November 1979): 48.

Michaud, Roland. *Caravans to Tartary*. New York: Viking Press, 1978.

Moeller, Walter O. "The Felt Shops of Pompeii." In *American Journal of Archaeology* 75, no. 2 (April 1971): 188–89.

Oliver, Paul, ed. *Encyclopedia of Vernacular Architecture of the World*. Cambridge: Cambridge University Press, 1997.

Olschki, L., *The Myth of Felt*. Berkeley and Los Angeles: University of California Press, 1949.

Róna-Tas, A. "Felt-making in Mongolia." In *Acta Orientalia Academiae Scientiarum Hungaricae*, 16 (1963): 199–215.

Rorex, Robert, and Wen Fong. *Eighteen Songs of a Nomad Flute: The Story of Lady Wen-Chi*. New York: Metropolitan Museum of Art, 1974.

Rowe, Anne Pollard, et al. "Felt Hat Making in Highland Ecuador." In *The Textile Museum Journal* 42/43 (2003–04): 114–19.

Ruyak, Jacqueline. "The Felt Frontier II, Jorie Johnson: Felt as Matrix." In *Surface Design Journal* 28, no. 4 (Summer 2004): 39–43.

———. "Mitsuko Tarui: A Feltmaker in Tokyo." In *Fiberarts* 28, no. 2 (September/October 2001): 18.

Ryder, M. L. "The Origin of Felt-making and Spinning." In *Antiquity: a Quarterly Review of Archaeology* 36, no. 144 (December 1962): 304.

Steinkeller, Piotr. "Mattresses and Felt in Early Mesopotamia." In *Oriens Antiquus* 19, no. 2 (1980): 79–100.

Thomas, Katharina. *Filz: Kunst, Kunsthandwerk, und Design*, exh. cat. Stuttgart: Arnoldsche, 2000.

Tsagareli, N. *Georgian Decorative Thick Felt*. Tbilisi: Khelovneba Publishing House, 1972.

Turnau, Irena. *Hand Felting in Europe and Asia: From the Middle Ages to the 20th Century*. Warsaw: Instytut Archeologii I Etnologii, 1997.

Westfall, Carol D. "Contemporary Feltmakers." In *Shuttle, Spindle & Dyepot* 36, no. 3, issue 143 (Summer 2005): 31–37.

Ziek, Bhakti. "The Felt Frontier I, Polly Stirling: Contemporary Feltmaker." In *Surface Design Journal* 28, no. 4 (Summer 2004): 35–38.

Selected Index

Acknowledgments

Cooper-Hewitt, National Design Museum is grateful to the following individuals and organizations for their assistance and support during the preparation of the *Fashioning Felt* exhibition and catalogue.

Exhibition Lenders
521 Design: Chris Ferebee, Laurice Parkin
American Museum of Natural History:
Samantha Alderson, John Hansen, Dr. Laurel Kendall, Kristen Mable, Mary Lou Murillo
Andrea Rosen Gallery: Teneille Haggard, Laurel Jensen
Tord Boontje
Louise Campbell
Cappellini
Cassina: Pui-Pui Li
Brigit Daamen
Diller Scofidio + Renfro: David Allen, Eamon Tobin
Tom Dixon: Tom Dixon, Alice Foster
Drud & Koppe Gallery
E. F. Walter, Inc.
Pernelle Fagerlund
FELT Studio: Kathryn Walter
Flocks: Christien Meindertsma
Lene Frantzen
Mehmet Gircic
Hay
Herat Carpets: Shir and Parvis Paiwand
Hive UK: Monika Piatkowski
Françoise Hoffmann
Hut Up: Christine Birkle
JA Felt: Janice Arnold, Keli Butler, Bettie Edwards, Camille Fastle, Emily Iyall, Margaret Jones, Loren Klyne, Vanessa Lang, Blake Lugar, Barb McConkey, Brittany Mroczek, Michael Riotto, Pam Sinclair-Nixon, Pat Wald, Bianca Weber, Lauren Winstead
Jorie Johnson
Claudy Jongstra: Claudy Jongstra, Marleen Engbersen, Wendy Gooren, Jellie Tichelaar
LAMA: Yvonne Laurysen, Erik Mantel
Inge Lindqvist
Majken Mann and Nynne Faerch
Christine Martens
Ben Mickus
molo: Stephanie Forsythe, Todd MacAllen
Molteni: Massimo Citterio
Clifton Monteith
The Museum of Modern Art: Paola Antonelli, Paul Galloway
Nanimarquina: Ariadna Rousaud
Jean Nouvel
Odegard: Stephanie Odegard, Angela Attento
Gaetano Pesce
Christophe Pillet
Porro: Milena Cassotti
Ruckstuhl: Peter Ruckstuhl, Jutta Bernhardt
Skulpturfabriken: Stina Lindholm
Alexander van Slobbe
SUP Design: Søren Ulrik Petersen
Ilkka Suppanen
Ursula Suter
Yeohlee Teng: Yeohlee Teng, Robert Barr
The Textile Museum: Sumru Belger Krody, Esther Méthé
Textile Museum of Canada: Nataley Nagy, Natalie Nekrassova, Roxane Shaughnessy
Andrea Zittel

Other Support
Asian Cultural Council
Brand Felts: Jack Brand
Creative Engineering
Nick Foley
The Fulbright Scholar Program
Michael Gervers
Stan Klyne
KPFF Consulting Engineers: Caroline Weiss, Amber Owen
Material Connexion: George Beylerian
Paul Moore
Oceanic Graphic Printing: David Li, Michael Lok, Barbara Zee
The Spence School: Bodie Brizendine

Design Team
Book design: Pure+Applied: Paul Carlos, Urshula Barbour, Carolyn Thomas
Installation design: Toshiko Mori Architect: Toshiko Mori, Jolie Kerns, Phoebe Springstubb
Graphic design: Tsang Seymour Design: Patrick Seymour, Catarina Tsang, Andrew Hardy
Lighting design: Mary Ann Hoag

At Cooper-Hewitt
Communications and Marketing: Jennifer Northrop, William Berry, Laurie Olivieri
Conservation: Lucy Commoner, Sarah Scaturro
Development and External Affairs: Caroline Baumann, Deborah Ahn, Sophia Amaro, Joanna Broughton, Deborah Fitzgerald, Kelly Mullaney, Barbara Roan
Education: Caroline Payson, Shamus Adams, Mei Mah, Erin McCluskey, Alexander Tibbets
Exhibitions: Mathew O'Connor, Mathew Weaver, and the installation crew
Finance: Christopher Jeannopoulos
Master's Fellow: Laura Camerlengo
OFEO: Steve Roth, Janice Slivko
Operations: Diane Galt
Registrar: Steven Langehough, Melanie Fox, Wendy Rogers, Bethany Romanowski, Larry Silver

Photographic Credits
All photographic credits are included in the image captions. Cooper-Hewitt, National Design Museum is grateful to the organizations and individuals credited for their permission to reproduce images in this book. Every effort has been made to trace and contact the copyright holders of the images reproduced; any errors or omissions shall be corrected in subsequent editions.

Copyright

FASHIONING FELT
Susan Brown, Andrew Dent, Christine Martens,
and Matilda McQuaid
© 2009 Smithsonian Institution

Published by
Cooper-Hewitt, National Design Museum
Smithsonian Institution
2 East 91st Street
New York, NY 10128, USA
www.cooperhewitt.org

Published on the occasion of the exhibition
Fashioning Felt
at Cooper-Hewitt, National Design Museum,
Smithsonian Institution,
March 6–September 7, 2009.

Fashioning Felt is made possible by the generous support of

The exhibition is also funded in part by
The Coby Foundation, Ltd.

and the Mondriaan Foundation

Support for the Claudy Jongstra installation is provided by
Elise Jaffe + Jeffrey Brown.

Additional support is provided by
The Netherland-America Foundation and
The Consulate General of Switzerland in New York.

This publication is made possible in part by
The Andrew W. Mellon Foundation.

Distributed to the trade worldwide by
Assouline Publishing
601 West 26th Street, 18th floor
New York, NY 10001, USA
www.assouline.com

First edition: March 2009

ISBN: 978-0-910503-89-1

Library of Congress Control Number: 2009921596

Museum Editor: Chul R. Kim, Director of Publications

Design: Pure+Applied, New York

Printed in China by Oceanic Graphic Printing.